A PRIVATE EDUCATION
WITHOUT THE FEES?

A PRIVATE EDUCATION WITHOUT THE FEES?

*How to give your child the
best start in life for free*

Cheryl Salmon

A Private Education Without the Fees?
How to give your child the best start in life for free

First published in the United Kingdom in 2019
by Cavalcade Books
www.cavalcadebooks.com

ISBN 978-1-9996213-3-9

Cover design by Colourburst Lithographic Ltd
www.colourburst.com

This book is dedicated to my own parents,
David Walter James White and Flora White (now Hawtree).

From the bottom of my heart, thank you.

Contents

Introduction

HOW I NEARLY GOT THUMPED

I was in a local market one Saturday when I heard a man's voice nearby raised in anger. He had a small boy aged about two with him. He was kneeling next to the child and smacking his bottom and saying, "Stop crying!" Obviously, hitting the mite just made him cry more. I was filled with anger at his treatment of this tiny child and went over and said, in my best teacher "telling-off" voice: "What do you think you are doing?! How do you think hitting him will help?"

The man looked up, astonished to be spoken to in that way, and then stood up. He was a well-built youngish man and quite a bit taller than me. With a thunderous expression on his face, he glowered over me and said menacingly: "Will you mind your own business, please?!"

Still angry, I said, "Well actually this **is** my business. When people treat their children badly, as you are, I usually have to sort out their problems in school!" He was somewhat astonished at this riposte; and because he was caught a bit off balance, before he had time to reply or do anything else I walked off into the crowd.

Looking back, I can see that this young father did not really understand how to be an effective parent. It is likely that as a child he had experienced the sort of parenting he was dishing out himself, and had no idea what could help his son develop properly and happily.

Personally, I am passionately committed to helping children fulfil their potential, to be happy and feel safe. As in the situation mentioned above, I have sometimes felt an overwhelming need to intervene in situations where children are not being nurtured or treated well. This "desire to interfere" has caused my own daughters embarrassment and on this particular occasion got me into a fairly tricky situation…

I interfered because I believe that **parenting is the most important job in the world**. I have worked for 40 years in the education sector, most recently in primary schools, but also with all age ranges, including 16-19-year-olds and young offenders. However, I still regard my most important role as having been a parent (and now a grandparent). Children are, after all, our future. Giving them the best chances of success in life is all-important; and parenting shapes the attitudes, self-belief and potential of all children. As parents, we all have the absolute power to shape a child's future in a positive or negative way.

This book is about how to give your child the best start in life. It presents simple, practical – and costless – parenting techniques that work.

Not only do I believe that parenting is the most important job in the world, **it can also be the best and most**

rewarding job in the world. My aim in this book is to put the most important aspects of everything I have learned as a professional and as a parent into the form of practical advice that might be useful to all parents, whatever their background or location. This advice brings together some ideas and recommendations that I believe can help parents to give their child at least the same advantages as those conferred by an expensive private education. (Arguably, some of the principles will be just as useful for those who are already paying independent school fees; and it is also possible that some of what follows could give your children **more** advantages than an independent fee-paying education.) I have deliberately tried to keep the advice presented here clear, simple and straightforward. Most of my suggestions have no costs attached, apart from the resources of your time and effort, which **will** be rewarded.

WANTING THE BEST FOR OUR CHILDREN

Most of us picture ourselves becoming parents, whether that works out for us or not. Childlessness is rising statistically, but 2015 Office of National Statistics (ONS) figures still showed the vast majority (83%) of women at age 45 as having had children. And as parents, almost all of us will love our children. Although, sometimes we'll find the challenges of being a parent demanding and even frustrating – those sleepless nights when they're little (and maybe again later when they're teenagers), the worries about their safety, the cost of child care, balancing being a parent with earning money, that interesting time when the hormones hit (and suddenly they realise that if they don't do what you say, the sky won't fall in)... The list goes on and on.

As parents, we'll all say we want the best for our children, although what "the best" looks like varies hugely between different communities and families. Having spent most of my career in schools, working with children from the age of three to young adults, I found it fascinating to see how family circumstances and attitudes influence children's happiness, success and life chances.

NO ONE KNOWS ALL THE ANSWERS

In spite of all the TV programmes and books out there, no one knows all the answers about parenting, and not every case is as clear cut as the one I've just mentioned – there is not necessarily a right and a wrong thing to do in every situation. I know and have worked, personally and professionally, with lots of different people who are parents. They all have their own take on parenting and most people are successful, in the sense that their children reach adulthood reasonably healthy and well-adjusted, as well as financially secure. There is no perfect way to be a parent, but there are parenting techniques that do and don't work.

IMPROVING HAPPINESS

I do have a fundamental belief that as parents we can all take action which will improve the general level of wellbeing and happiness and remove the sources of unhappiness and underachievement, not just specifically in our children, but because children are our future, in society as a whole. In my career I have derived great satisfaction from helping children and their families to achieve changes which made them happier and more successful. If we shape our children's future in a positive way – through the way our parenting shapes attitudes, self-belief and potential – we will benefit all of society, not just our own children.

TALKING TO PARENTS

As a professional working in the education sector, I have spent a lot of time talking to parents. This isn't to say that I haven't learnt a great deal too from teachers, instructors and support staff – all with their own special skills, insights, experiences and talents – and from children themselves, including my own, and from various professional courses I have attended; but talking and working with parents has provided me with particular insights that inform this book. Often, I have been involved in talking with parents when there has been a family crisis, or when a child has had behaviour problems, or where there was a concern about a child's safety or wellbeing. Quite often I found myself repeating the same suggestions or advice, and over the years I have been gratified to see some really good impact for children as a result of how parents have listened and changed their parenting practice.

Specifically for this book, I have supplemented this professional experience with a number of interviews undertaken with parents from a range of different backgrounds. You will find quotations from these interviews scattered throughout this book. Where the parents in question have been happy for me to do so, I have given their real first names. In every case, many thanks go to these helpful mums and dads who agreed to be interviewed for the book.

I'll end this introduction with a quote from one of those parents, Elaine, who echoed my belief that parenting can be the best and most rewarding job in the world by saying, "Cheryl, I've had a ball!"

Chapter 1
PARENTING AND WHY IT MATTERS

WHAT IS PARENTING ALL ABOUT?

What is **parenting all about**? Let's begin with some comments about expectations and experience from some of the parents I interviewed for this book.

What do you expect before you become a parent?

"Your attitude is different before you have children. When you have them, your world changes and you become determined to protect them from anything." (Isabel)

"Before I had them I didn't realise that your whole life would revolve about them... the most frustrating thing is not being able to fix it when things go wrong for them." (Elaine)

"I didn't realise that your children are very much their own people. They will not necessarily act and think as you do." (Alice)

"It was difficult discovering that they are their own person, not a blank page you can fiddle with... I didn't realise that sleep was a luxury." (Stella)

"I didn't realise that having children would mean so little sleep. It opens up a new pain receptor in the brain." (Nigel)

"I had no experience of babies… I was looking forward to having a baby. I thought she would be like a little rosebud. I had no idea it would be so challenging." (Flora)

"I recommend being a parent; It's a fulfilling learning experience." (Russell)

"It doesn't matter how much people give you advice, you don't know what it's like until you experience it." (Helen)

"Before I was a parent, I didn't realise that how to be a good parent was not obvious – you are not given a manual!" (Philippe)

"It has softened me up. I'm more interested in different views – being a parent speeds up your maturity and development." (Alex)

"I didn't realise my time wouldn't be my own again." (John)

"The most difficult thing was constantly worrying. I was paranoid about health, accidents etc. I didn't realise you could love somebody more than yourself." (Jenny)

"It is difficult to find time to do things around the house, DIY, gardening etc. because [children] need so much time and attention. I didn't realise I could love them unconditionally, even if they scratch your car! I realised that material things don't compare to my children." (Richard)

"It's difficult juggling parenting with work because you need flexibility and you need to be available to your children. There is a lot of pressure on parents in terms of competition and criticism." (Helen A)

BEING PARENTED AFFECTS YOU

So, there are surprises in becoming a parent. It opens your eyes to all sorts of feeling and experiences, many of which you weren't expecting. But even before we become parents ourselves, we all experience being parented in a unique way, and the range of ways is very diverse – from being, say, an abandoned child parented by the state or a charity to being a long-awaited only child, or even the ninth or tenth child in a large family.

Everyone reading this book will have had a unique experience which has given them ideas about the quality of parenting they have received. Many, like me, will appreciate that they had a privileged experience and that their own parents did their best in their particular circumstances to provide a loving family setting to nurture their children and prepare them for life's challenges. Others among us may feel let down or even embittered by the quality of parenting they received. No one would argue against the idea that poor parenting, abuse and neglect often damages children and adversely affects their likelihood of a successful future.

DO YOU MAKE IT UP AS YOU GO ALONG?

It is somewhat astonishing to think of the cost, effort and training which has to go into allowing someone to legally drive a car on the road, and yet there is no recognised training or qualification needed to become a parent – apart from a functioning reproductive system!

This means that most people learn how to become parents by replicating the parenting they have experienced (although some, unhappy with their own childhood experiences, consciously change their own parenting in response). Most make it up as they go along, influenced by friends, family and the media. As well as our own personal experiences of parenting being a factor, society has changed greatly over the course of recent decades, and this has had a huge impact on family lives and relationships.

EQUAL OPPORTUNITIES – HOW WE'VE CHANGED

The changes in attitudes and social situations over the last 50 years have been huge. Along with more frequent family changes, people's values and attitudes have evolved out of all recognition. Many of today's young adults would find it hard to believe that it is less than a century ago (1928) since all women were given the right to vote. Milestones like the 1970 Equal Pay Act (making it illegal to pay women lower rates of pay than men for the same work) and the 1975 Sex Discrimination Act (making it illegal to discriminate against women in work, education and training) have helped usher in an era where roles are no longer seen as exclusively male or female. And although we live in a world where the gender pay gap is still an issue and where women are still under-represented in senior roles in many professions, we no longer live in one where we would be surprised to see a female bus driver or male nurse.

Men who choose to stay at home to be the main home support and child carer while their wife or partner earns the money are much more common than they were even 20 years ago. (In the UK, ONS statistics gave the number of stay-at-home fathers in 2014 as 229,000, up from 111,000 in 1993.) This can only be a positive thing.

Carey: *It's certainly heading in the right direction, although there are still some jobs where men are paid more than women.*

RESPECT FOR ALL RACES

We have also moved on in our attitudes towards racial equality. Many of today's young adults would find it hard to believe that racist language was treated as being an acceptable part of mainstream television entertainment as recently as the 1970s and 1980s, or that 1987 was the first year that four black MPs were elected. Milestones like the 1976 Race Relations Act (which made both direct and indirect discrimination an offence) and the 1999 McPherson Report (which, in the wake of the investigation of the murder of Stephen Lawrence, found the

Metropolitan Police to be institutionally racist) have helped usher in an era where racism in all forms is increasingly no longer tolerated. And although, as with women's rights, we live in a world where progress still needs to be made in significant areas, fewer and fewer people in modern Britain find any form of racism socially acceptable.

DISABILITY RIGHTS

Similarly, progress has been made in terms of equal rights for disabled people. The landmark 1995 Disability Discrimination Act made it illegal to discriminate against disabled people in connection with employment or the provision of goods, facilities and services. The 2012 Paralympic Games in London were the largest Paralympics to date with athletes with disabilities having unprecedented media focus and celebration of their successes.

On the academic front, there was international admiration for the late Professor Steven Hawking. We recognised him as a genius in his specialism of astrophysics, in spite of him suffering from a debilitating and progressive medical condition which kept him dependent on carers and specialist equipment to help him move, communicate and live. In the twenty-first century, changes in the law now promote and protect the employment rights of disabled people like Professor Hawking.

LGBT RIGHTS

The past 50 years have also seen a sea change in attitudes towards lesbian, gay, bisexual and transgender people. Homosexual acts between males had been illegal in the UK until 1967 saw their partial decriminalisation in England and Wales. And although it took until 2001 for the age of consent for homosexual acts to be equalised with that for heterosexual acts, recent years have seen a raft of measures that promote LGBT rights including Gordon Brown's 2009 public apology for the way in which Alan Turing (the computer genius who solved the Enigma code in World War Two) was treated for being gay after the War, and the legalisation of same-sex marriage in 2014. Happily, we now live in a world where we accept the likes of MPs and sportspeople, and not just those in the entertainment industry, being openly gay.

UNINTENDED CONSEQUENCE?

These changes in the equal opportunities agenda are very positive and an indication of how our culture has matured. Every child growing up should believe that their potential is not hampered by their gender, race, disability or sexual identity. However, I do wonder if there is an unintended side-effect in our society which is not all positive. Have our parenting skills been affected by our cultural shift towards equality? Perhaps there is an unintended consequence that the culture of respect for others, which we can and should wholeheartedly endorse, has led to a misplaced and over-respectful attitude towards the child, which is not always conducive to good parenting, and that some parents have **lost their confidence as adults in their relationships with their children**.

WHO IS IN CHARGE?

In common with most of my generation, as a child in the 1950s and 60s I knew exactly who was in charge in our family – it was definitely my mother and father and all of us understood that. I went through the usual hormone-inspired stroppiness as an adolescent, but remember very clearly, having given my mother a bit of "backchat", my father's stern and quite angry response: "Don't you dare speak to my wife like that!"

Nowadays, we witness challenges by quite young children to parental authority when out and about and maybe even in our own families. We have all witnessed children who are rude or even aggressive towards their parents, especially those of us who have worked in schools. For my generation, this can come as a shock, and personally I believe it can actually be dangerous to the wellbeing and development of the child.

COMMUNITIES WHERE PARENTS ARE RESPECTED

In some communities, both in the UK and abroad, the tradition of parental authority is much stronger than in others – respect for the parents and other older members of the family and the adult community is much more strongly embedded, and challenging that authority can lead to disgrace or ostracism. It is interesting to note that in those communities where there still remains a tradition of respect for parents, the children are much more likely to succeed in education, and may well go on to reach higher levels of educational attainment than their parents.

SOME FACTS AND FIGURES

South Asians make up only 5.5% of England's population and Chinese only 0.7% of the population (2011 UK Census) and yet Indian and Chinese teenagers are the highest achievers by the time they reach 16 years old and take their GCSE exams. I think there are two reasons for this. First, Indian and Chinese parents believe strongly in the value of education and are determined that their children will achieve their best at school – they have the highest of expectations. Second, in my experience parents in these communities tend to still maintain authority over their children in the home – what they say, goes. I'm not saying this leads to 100% happiness always, but it definitely seems to help youngsters do well at school.

The controversial and fascinating book on parenting by Amy Chua, *Battle Hymn of the Tiger Mother*, provides a powerful insight into Chinese parenting traditions, especially as regards aspirations, determination and success in all you do. Maybe this provides the reasons for the outstanding academic performance of Chinese children in our schools.

HAVE PARENTS BECOME MORE UNCERTAIN?

So why are things so different with children of other backgrounds? Has something changed about the way children respond to their parents' authority? And if so, how has this come about? Perhaps in part it is connected to the way our society has matured and the much stronger general acceptance of equal rights. Perhaps it is because some parents, fully aware of and committed to equal rights, feel uncertain about their own authority with their children. They might think that their child should have equal rights or status with them in terms of controlling everyday life and choices. Sometimes they even share information about their personal relationships with young children, as if they were an adult friend or companion.

YOUR CHILD CAN'T BE YOUR MATE

This attempt by parents to put a child on the same level as themselves can mean the parent does not feel comfortable in asserting parental authority, which can be a difficult and even dangerous situation. ("Stop at the edge of the pavement!" "Maybe I will, maybe I won't"…) A small child does not have enough experience of life to make a judgement about what she* should do or not do. Relationships between adults and children should, of course, be based on mutual respect, but the adult has to be "in charge" to ensure that the child is safe (physically and emotionally). Also, children cannot just **instinctively** know what is expected of them in society as regards values, behaviour and moral choices. We need to shape their thinking, behaviour and attitudes in a way that provides them with the best social advantages and opportunities. We need to provide guidance and direction so that they can be happy and successful.

RULES AND BOUNDARIES

As we'll discuss in more detail in the next chapter, there are many reasons why parents choose an independent education, but one of them is because they believe it provides a formal setting in which it is clear who is in charge and what the rules and boundaries are. The understanding of a hierarchy and how to operate successfully within it is critical for a successful future. (An apprentice or office junior who tries to see themselves as equal to their boss usually learns the error of their ways quite quickly!)

---

* Rather than use the singular "they" which might be confusing, I use "she" in this book as the default pronoun for the child. This can be read as "she or he" and shouldn't be taken to mean I'm referring exclusively to girls.

IF YOU ALWAYS BACK UP YOUR CHILD

The other consideration is how parents relate to others involved with their child – especially teachers and other school staff. There is a natural instinct to want to protect your child, but a few parents feel that if their child is unhappy about something which has happened at school (being kept in at playtime for upsetting another child, for example) it is their role to defend their child regardless of the rights or wrongs of the situation. A YouGov poll published in June 2017 showed that if there was a behaviour problem with their child, older parents were much more likely to accept the teacher's point of view, but 42% overall didn't know how they would react. This can create difficulties because if a child gets the idea that her parent will defend whatever she does, it removes a sense of personal responsibility for her actions and gives out a mixed message about acceptable behaviour, which can be very confusing and can often lead to further behaviour problems.

LITTLE GIRLS AND FRIENDSHIPS

It's also worth noting that children go through different stages where they "try out" different ways of relating to other children and to adults. In particular, little girls can become extremely skilled at manipulating the opinions of the adults close to them. Primary teachers will tell you how common it is for them to get into tricky and upsetting situations at school where friendships fluctuate and change on a day-to-day (or hour-to-hour!) basis.

Because they become very involved in social situations between the ages of, say, six to nine, little girls become adept at painting a picture of a situation which reflects them in a positive light... but may not be the whole story. So, it can go like this:

Mum picks up eight-year-old daughter, Rosie, from school. In the car, on the way home...

ROSIE (bursts into tears): Mum, Shanna isn't my friend any more! She's picking on me and being really mean!

MUM: Oh, that's terrible, darling! It's bullying! I will come into school and sort it out tomorrow.

Rosie spends the evening looking dramatically downcast and tearful. At the dinner table, her older brother Sam (ten-years-old) offers to beat up Shanna at playtime.

That night on the Facebook parents' page for the school, lots of side-taking and online discussion takes place about who said what to whom, who was most upset and how terrible it is that the school let it happen.

The next day, just before registration, Mum storms into the classroom.

MUM (to class teacher): My daughter Rosie is being bullied by Shanna! I thought this school was supposed to have an anti-bullying policy! What are you doing about it?

TEACHER: Oh, I think they had a falling out yesterday. I'll investigate and let you know what we find out.

MUM: Well, I want that bully Shanna excluded! (storms out of classroom)

The teacher investigates and discovers that Shanna has become friendly with a new girl in the class. Rosie is not happy about this and is feeling left out and jealous. She has told Shanna she is mean and ugly, and has big feet. Shanna has responded by saying Rosie has horrible frizzy hair and then flounced off with her new friend.

The teacher discusses the problem with the two girls, and they agree that it is OK to have new friends, but you mustn't be mean to old friends. The teacher writes a note for Rosie's mum to let her know it has been resolved and keeps a careful eye on who sits where and playground issues for a week or two.

This might be the end of the issue, but probably won't be...

ANYTHING GOES

Another major change in our society is how we have adopted an "anything goes" attitude to family life. Fifty years ago, the "rules" of family life and parenting were fairly clearly laid out. The ideal situation was as follows (although I recognise this was not the case for all families, and nor am I presenting this as an ideal for today): people married before having children; Dad went out to earn money; Mum stayed at home and looked after the children;

the moral compass was provided by the church, school assemblies and religious education (RE) classes and, broadly speaking, children did as they were told. Now things are not as cut and dried: many children are born to parents who are not married; because of the rise in the divorce rate and the loss of stigma associated with it, "re-formed" families are much more common than they were, so children need to adapt to a range of stepfamily relationships. The *Daily Telegraph* (8th May 2014) reported that a total of 4.2 million children in England and Wales – 35% – do not live with both parents. The article also put the number of unmarried couples now raising children as having jumped by 37% in a decade to just over one million.

This means that today more children are living with changes in their parenting arrangements. Most people have friends who have been married or in a relationship (with children), then were single parents for a period, and then perhaps cohabited with a new partner and their own and the new partner's children. So, we (both parents and children) are living through a period where big changes in family life are common.

IN THE OLD DAYS, IT WAS SCANDALOUS

We used to be scandalised by the idea of sex before marriage, whereas now the media celebrates flexible views of morality (e.g. who is sleeping with whom on the celebrity circuit) and there is a broad spectrum of information and opinions on what effective parenting should look like. These are available through TV, books, magazines and the internet (look, for example, into the debates that can be found online about how often you should pick up your baby if she cries). Sometimes the views of a celebrity, without any professional skills or qualifications (or previous experience) in childrearing, education or psychology, who has recently become a parent, are touted around in magazines almost as if they are "expert advice". Because family members are often spread about across the country, quite often guidance and help from experienced parents is no longer close at hand. Without the common boundaries and recommendations about childrearing which used to be accepted without question, it's not surprising that some parents feel a bit lost and get themselves into difficult situations which make life harder.

PARENTS WANT THEIR CHILDREN TO BE HAPPY AND DO WELL

Education in the UK public, or state, sector has changed hugely over the last 50 years, and the pace of how schools are expected to change has shifted up a number of gears. Changes in government policy have had a huge impact on schools in the public sector. Our schools have become much more autonomous, but also much more accountable through inspection and parent power – where information about children's achievement is publicly and easily available online.

PARENT POWER

Parents are now seen as consumers and customers whose preferences influence the financial status of schools and what Ofsted (the Office for Standards in Education, Children's Services and Skills – the body responsible for inspecting state schools) inspections report. School budgets are strongly influenced by how many children they educate, so the more people who choose to send a child to a particular school, the more money the school's budget gets and the better its reputation, creating a sort of marketing strategy. This has had a number of effects – it is well known that parental preference for particular schools actually influences the price of houses in its catchment area. An online report by Harry Yorke in April 2017 noted the following:

"A survey of more than one million homes across England has revealed that parents are paying vast property premiums to move home, with the average house in outstanding school catchment area costing £52,000 more on average than those near schools which require improvement."

This shows that many parents who may not be willing or able to pay school fees for an independent education and are keeping their children at state schools are nonetheless effectively prepared to pay out extra financial costs to ensure that their child has a place at a school which they perceive to offer a better education. Parents have even been known to use a friend or relative's address in order to gain a place for their child at the school they prefer.

SCHOOL AND PARENTS IN PARTNERSHIP

Why does all this matter? It matters because children benefit hugely from their parents working **in partnership** with the school. The government produced a report in 2008 about the difference it makes to children when their parents are involved with their school and one of its main findings was that: "Parental involvement in children's education from an early age has a significant effect on educational achievement, and continues to do so into adolescence and adulthood". The issue of how parents can ensure they get the most for their child from their state education is discussed in some detail in Chapter 8 "Making the most of the education you already pay for".

Independent schools, of course, offer an alternative to the state sector for those able to pay. In the next chapter we address the question: why are many parents not satisfied with state schools and so opt to pay school fees?

Chapter 2
WHY PARENTS PAY FOR A PRIVATE EDUCATION

BOARDING SCHOOL?

Over the last ten years in the UK and US, as well as in a huge range of other countries, there has been a huge amount of attention on one fictional school. It is a boarding school set in a lovely, old traditional gothic building. The teachers all wear academic gowns. There is a strict uniform policy, and all the children compete to gain house points for their houses. This school is, of course, Hogwarts in JK Rowling's Harry Potter books. Perhaps one of the reasons for the huge success of the series is the idealised depiction of many people's image of a successful independent school (which, to the puzzlement of those outside the UK, we call "public schools").

> **Stella:** *I think they're fine. If people want to spend the money on their children's education, it's up to them. It also provides extra capacity in the state system.*

HOW MANY PAY?

In the UK about 628,000 children are educated privately in about 2,600 schools; this is about 7% of the children of school age in the population (Independent Schools Council Census 2016). For some fairly comfortably-off parents the cost of private education is not a particular challenge. (There is a huge range, but the Independent Schools Council survey says that it now costs more than £30,000 to send a child to boarding school for a year, and it's £15,500 a year to send a child to a private day school). So, for less well-off parents it means giving up holidays, a larger home or a newer car to pay school fees with the intention of buying their child or children a flying start in life.

Helen: *If a parent can afford it, I think it's great – they get a more varied education and become more successful.*

In the UK, free education has been a right for all children since 1891. The quality of state education has improved dramatically as measured by exam results in all age groups. In spite of this, many parents feel that they are providing their offspring with special advantages through paying fees for an independent education. So, what is it about independent education that remains so attractive and for some parents is seen as an essential responsibility to ensure their child's future?

> **Darren:** *I think because you're paying, you expect a better service and the best results, like better grades and improved prospects.*

HIGHLY-PAID PROFESSIONS

One of the main advantages is a social or networking one. If it is true that when jobseeking it's not what you know but who you know, then many parents recognise that networking with the right social groups opens doors to their offspring. In the last few years there has been publicity about unpaid internships giving some graduates a head start in certain businesses. These voluntary posts are often not even advertised, but become available through family, social or school connections. The Sutton Trust report "Leading People" published in 2016 describes how in certain professions those who have attended independent schools are a significantly higher proportion than might be expected: 74% of judges and other senior members of the judiciary, 61% of top doctors, 48% of top civil servants and 32% of MPs have all been privately educated. If access to opportunities to have a career in these well-paid professions were spread equally, it would be expected that only a maximum of 7% of each group would be privately educated.

> **Peter:** *I think independent schools give children more verbal stimulation.*

SCHOOLS GET MONEY TO IMPROVE EQUALITY

The government has recognised for many years now the gap between children from underprivileged and relatively well-off background in terms of exam success. As a result, state schools get extra money in their budgets (currently known as "Pupil Premium") to spend on helping children from less well-off backgrounds. The Pupil Premium is paid in respect of children who qualify, or have qualified in the recent past, for free school meals, or who have been looked after under local authority care.

This funding is expected to help those children from less wealthy backgrounds catch up with children from better-off parents.

> **John:** *One of my children was very bright, and needed stretching, as private schools can.*

It is very positive that the government sees the importance of narrowing the gap between disadvantaged and middle-class children, allocates extra school funding to this and requires schools to report on how effectively they use it. Schools are also judged in inspections on how effective they are in ensuring that underprivileged children make good progress compared to those from higher-income families. Unfortunately, there is still a huge gap between the two groups of children in how well they do in terms of qualifications and income as adults.

ACADEMIC RESULTS

> **Richard**: *Private schools are businesses. I don't object to them, although they are elitist. I choose where I shop, so why not?*

It has long been known that where academic exam results are used as the measure of success, such as access to undergraduate degrees, private education delivers the goods. Children who are privately educated are four times as likely to gain straight A grades at A level as those in state education (and only 0.5% of children on free school meals do). Another indicator is that two-fifths of Oxbridge undergraduates come from the 7% of children who are privately educated (*The Observer* 12th December 2015 – quoting the Social Mobility and Child Poverty Commission annual report).

As already mentioned, independently educated people are much more likely to be appointed to the top jobs in many fields, quite often having graduated from Oxbridge. (40% of top doctors went to Oxbridge, as did 26% of MPs.)

Philippe: *I think the social view of those in independent schools is narrow.*

The Independent Schools Council's figures show that many parents pay for private education in the last two years of full-time education before transfer to university, since this has a clear impact on the grades attained in A Levels, which are so important to get into the most competitive universities (Oxford, Cambridge and others in the Russell Group, a group which comprises 24 of the UK's leading universities). While many independent schools do have special schemes to help pay the school fees of children whose parents can't afford them, independent schools still do not include children from the full range of ability or background (unlike state schools). This means it is difficult to claim that independent schools are more successful at enabling their pupils to achieve well academically (because you aren't comparing like with like).

Liz: *My son is dyslexic and I looked at independent schools, but with the state schools he went to we were very lucky — he didn't lose out at all.*

SOCIAL SKILLS AND GOOD MANNERS

An independent education provides a set of values and codes which opens doors and promotes competitive skills and self-belief. Conventions of politeness and manners give clues about a person even before they have been able to promote their own skills and achievements to a recruiting manager. The person with the power to appoint or reject, as well as making a judgement or personally reacting to an applicant, will also take a view on how this person will impact on the image of the organisation if appointed. Someone who doesn't understand the "code" expected – shaking hands, waiting to be invited to sit down, using formal, grammatically correct English rather than slang – is disadvantaged before they are even asked a question in an interview. Knowing how you are expected to dress in certain settings is also important if you are to look as if you will fit in.

FEELING AT HOME

On the other hand, a person who has had the schooling and social contact which provides them with an induction into what is expected of them in middle-class or professional social situations will usually be made to feel welcome and will quickly feel "at home" with the same codes of behaviour, giving them a flying start in a new work setting. High expectations of social skills and manners tend to be a feature of the curriculum in independent schools. For example, Woodbridge Independent School in Suffolk mentions its "Awards for Good Manners Week" and Hanford School (for girls) in Hambledon Hill in Dorset actively and overtly promotes good manners as part of its culture:

Hanford has always placed great importance on good manners. Over the years a system developed which is applied as each girls' manners improve. The system works on the principle of a ladder, with each rung on the "ladder" having a popular name attached.

As a girl arrives at Hanford she automatically starts near the bottom of the scale – and she is named a "Boa Constrictor". As her table manners improve she can get moved up, or if she does something dreadful she is moved down!

Every Friday, after lunch, the week's scores for manners are read out. (School website)

Quite reasonably, parents often believe that an independent education provides an induction into a privileged "closed shop" which promotes a strong sense of community based around agreed social codes like manners, language and vocabulary. There is good evidence that often in social situations (and therefore not just in the context of matters like recruitment mentioned above) we make judgements on what we feel about another person through social cues in the first few minutes of meeting them. For example, choosing the right clothes and shoes, knowing when to shake hands, when to stand up or sit down, the cutlery to use in a formal setting and even the correct use of spoken English – all give messages about our background which may or may not be received positively by others whom we meet.

ATTENTION AND CLASS SIZE

Many parents believe that their child will have a better quality of education in a school where classes are smaller than those typically found in the state sector. This is a controversial area as, according to Programme for International Student Assessment (PISA) data (which compares educational achievements across the world), the academic achievement of children in some other countries (e.g. China and South Korea) by the age of 15 is significantly higher than in the UK, yet children are in much larger classes. The average class size in a UK state primary is 24.5 children to one teacher; by comparison the average class size in an independent school is 11.5.

It seems to make sense that if a child has access to a 12th of the teacher's attention and time they should do better than a child who has less than half of that. Some studies (for example, The Tennessee Class Size Project in the 80s and 90s by Finn and Achilles, and "The Causal Effect of School Reform: Evidence from California's Quality Education Investment Act" by Burkander) have shown that children in smaller classes, especially younger children, achieve better academically and that this can have a long-term positive effect on attainment, especially for disadvantaged children. However, this contrasts with the conclusions of a significant Department for Education (DfE) report based on international comparisons between class sizes and pupil performance published in 2011. The "Class Size and Education in England Evidence Report" concluded that "there is no clear relationship between a country's average class size and attainment, suggesting that a country with a high-class size rank does not necessarily have a low attainment level." Also, as already mentioned, how do we explain that countries like China, South Korea and Singapore tend to have larger class sizes (48-55 pupils, 34+ pupils and 35+ pupils respectively) but also feature at the top of many international league tables for student performance? There are obviously other factors to consider such as parental support and motivation.

QUALITY OF TEACHING

The DfE report also refers to other evidence that it is the **quality** of teaching that has the most impact, rather than the amount of attention the child receives from the teacher; countries such as Finland are highly selective when appointing graduates to become teachers and make substantial investment in their professional development and training. Interestingly, many people don't realise that independent schools aren't obliged to have qualified teachers in the same way that state schools are required to have teachers who have Qualified Teacher Status (QTS) – which means they have passed a period of training and assessment and have an official registration with the Department for Education.

Other studies, such as the long-term Project STAR (for Student-Teacher Achievement Ratio) carried out in Tennessee, USA, say quite specifically that it is with the youngest children that small classes make the most difference (which perhaps fits with the suggestions about language development and its importance for academic success discussed later in Chapter 5 "Language, learning and thinking").

PARENTS FEEL SMALL CLASSES ARE BEST

Whatever the evidence, however, many parents feel that in an independent school with smaller classes their child will gain a more personalised experience and will receive more help with any learning problems, because of the extra focus and attention that their child receives.

OTHER WAYS TO BE SUCCESSFUL

In addition, most independent schools offer a range of extracurricular activities such as sports, music and drama which promote skills which are highly valued, such as confident public speaking or performing, competitive or team spirit, or leadership and communication skills. These provide a rich range of opportunities to be successful, often in state-of-the-art facilities, which build confidence in a range of ways.

For example, one school (Woodbridge) celebrates its range of provision online with the following information: "(Head's welcome): 'It also means developing creativity, empathy, the ability to think independently and work with others and above all the self-confidence to overcome any challenge. This may come from academic achievement, but for most students the activities they enjoy outside the classroom are just as important... The emphasis of the school is very much on what pupils can do well and ensuring they emerge happy, confident, well-balanced young men and women.'"

VALUES AND ASPIRATIONS

Many parents believe that a major advantage of an independent education is that their child will be in an atmosphere of high aspiration, where everyone is **expected** to do well, and where there is more focus on learning and higher levels of motivation. The view is that the child will be stretched in an environment with the ethos of high achievement and high expectations. Being with brighter or more intelligent children will "draw them along" and is said to produce a more competitive atmosphere which will promote motivation and effort.

> **Alice:** *I was completely conflicted about private education. I firmly believe in equal opportunities applying to education, but wouldn't be critical if I thought it was the best thing for the child. I think it gives most children an innate sense of entitlement, which can be positive, but can be also potentially restrictive.*

HIGH ASPIRATIONS

Here is a quote from the online prospectus of Kingsley

School, Royal Leamington Spa, illustrating this intention for their pupils:

Academically, girls are encouraged to have high aspirations. They develop a strong sense of belonging as they are expected to contribute to school life and participate in a wide range of enrichment opportunities. Girls leave Kingsley as confident, well-mannered, well-rounded and well-qualified young women ready to face the challenges of the adult world. Most of them continue their studies at the **university of their choice***.*

It's important to mention that not everyone who attends an independent school is happy about the quality of education they received.

Flora: *The early education I had at a private school was not of good quality. The people who were running it were doing it for the money – it was a peculiar set up. No doubt if I had gone to the local state school, I would've done much better. We did a lot of special writing, copying from the board. It was all about the presentation rather than the content – nice handwriting seemed to be very important.*

TRADITIONAL SUBJECTS

Some parents believe that independent schools value traditional subjects such as spelling and grammar. For example, one parent contributing to a discussion on Mumsnet, the online group for parents, explained how she believed that being taught at an independent school would guarantee that "your child would be taught by teachers who could spell and would teach children how to write and speak correctly". There is also no doubt that subjects like Latin are seen as more intellectually rigorous, have a certain cachet and are much more widely taught in independent than state schools.

> **Carey:** *If I was to find an independent school that fits with my views and preferences, I would definitely be prepared to pay for it. Ultimately if you pay for something, I believe you will get a better quality of service.*

WHICH CHILDREN HAVE BEHAVIOUR PROBLEMS?

Some parents feel that their child's education in the independent sector is less likely to be disrupted by bad behaviour from other children. This is for two reasons.

First, children with serious behaviour problems are more likely to come from lower social class households:

"Over the past half-century, social class inequality in the probability of an 11-year-old having a high level of conduct problems (in the top 10% of their cohort) has increased sharply. Working class children now appear nearly **four times as likely** to be among those with the worst conduct problems, compared with those from the most advantaged backgrounds. Similarly, the probability of an 11-year-old having a high level of emotional symptoms has become more closely linked to parental social class background, though the increase is less drastic. **In 1969 the social classes had actually been equal** in this respect. Hyperactivity shows a similar pattern, with slight inequality among those born in 1958, and higher levels since. Children of the unemployed or economically inactive (mostly in single-parent households) tend to fare worst in these areas, although we only have good data for the most recent generation." (Centre for Social Investigation, Nuffield College, Oxford, quoted by Lewis Anderson, February 2016)

Children from such backgrounds are unlikely to be attending independent schools.

Second, independent schools have more control over which children they keep as pupils if there is bad behaviour. Independent schools are not restricted from excluding children for bad behaviour in the way that state schools are.

PARENTAL ATTITUDES TO SCHOOL AND TEACHERS

Parents who pay for education are likely to give it a high priority and value. (After all, they are paying **twice** – once through their taxes for state education and again through their fees.) They are evidentially interested in education and the value it gives their child, and it is likely that the other parents at their child's school will have the same values. By contrast, in some state schools, a small minority of parents do not always value the education available to their child, as might be demonstrated by their inability to ensure good attendance at school, their unwillingness to support reading and homework, or their challenging attitude towards teachers and other school staff.

In May 2015 the *Daily Mirror* quoted Tonia Crosman, the headteacher of Emmer Green Primary School, as follows: "E-mails have been circulated or sent directly with abusive, personal comments about staff. I do not believe that this is the way to promote positive relationships and improve the school. It is in fact demoralising and unnecessary."

CODE OF CONDUCT FOR PARENTS

The same headteacher also provided a code of conduct for parents from the governing body which found the need to describe as "serious and unacceptable" the following types of behaviour:

- abusive and aggressive written correspondence

- using social media to publicly challenge school policies or discuss issues about individual children

- threatening behaviour

- physically or verbally intimidating staff

- using bad language or swearing to members of the school community

- breaching the school security procedures

It is worrying, but true, that many state school headteachers will have experienced some of this sort of behaviour from the parents of children at their school. This creates a number of challenges. Since the passing of the Local Management of Schools Act in 1988, a fundamental change has occurred in the role of parents and the nature of the power relationship between them and school staff.

PARENTS ARE CLIENTS OF THE SCHOOL

This is because that Act introduced the idea of parents as clients of the school, giving them the right to remove their children from a school and seek a place elsewhere if they were not satisfied with what was on offer. As the presence of each child adds a set amount of money to a school's budget, if numbers of children are removed from a school by their parents, it can create serious financial difficulties. So whereas before the Act was brought into law, headteachers didn't really have to take too much notice of parents' views and opinions (and I'm not saying that was right!), the opinions of parents about a school are taken very seriously nowadays by heads, governors and Ofsted inspectors. Quite appropriately, the parents are seen as the key customers, as they have the important (and potentially life-changing) decision to make on where to educate their child.

SOCIAL ATMOSPHERE

Another consideration is that if parents witness bad behaviour by other parents, they may not like the social atmosphere and experience for their own children. Also, critically, parents and teachers are likely to be very concerned if they witness bad behaviour and language from other adults on the school site because of the example set to their own children.

Some readers might be thinking "Well, why doesn't the head just exclude children with bad behaviour and their parents?" Well, the government, faced with a number of children who have been excluded due to poor behaviour and a reduction in places for specialist behaviour support (which is much more expensive to maintain for Local Authorities), has made it much more difficult and time-consuming to exclude children and parents who show aggressive behaviour by introducing complicated and bureaucratic appeals and recording processes.

"THE BEST SERVICE FOR MY CHILD"

On the other hand, independent schools have always experienced considerable pressure from parents. The National Education Union reported in 2018 that private school parents "are making private school teachers' lives 'insane' with their demands". Apparently, teachers are "at the beck and call of parents, governors and children who email them in the evenings and at weekends."

Some may take the attitude "I'm paying a lot of money, so I expect the best service for my child," and obviously the level of school fees means that if a parent is not happy, they can move their child to another independent school, so the school then loses the fees the parents were paying. It's not unknown for the parents to even sue the school!

However, independents are not subject to the same rules about exclusion as state schools, so it is much more straightforward and less time-consuming for them to "get rid" of difficult pupils. This makes it easier for independent schools to keep control of the behaviour of pupils and parents at their schools, which may lead to the view that independent school pupils are better behaved.

Carey: *Because the teachers are likely to be better paid, they are likely to be happier in the job, which will make them better teachers.*

IS IT JUST ABOUT EXAM SUCCESS?

The vast majority of parents (whether their children are in state or private schools) want the best for their children but are not necessarily sure about what "the best" looks like. We all know that doing well at school in academic terms (e.g. reaching "Expected" or "Exceeding" standards at the end of primary SATs tests, then going on to achieve at least five grades A*-C at GCSE) usually leads on to university and a successful career where you can earn a decent income. But what other information, experiences and values are required to help to ensure success in adult life? In my view, what a child comes to believe about herself and her relationships with other people in the world is very important for her future life chances. Let's think a little bit more about this in the next chapter.

Chapter 3
SELF-ESTEEM, CONFIDENCE AND POSITIVE THINKING

One of the attractions for parents choosing to send their children to independent schools is the promise of boosting their children's confidence. In the previous chapter, we saw the emphasis which independent schools place on this with websites saying how they develop confident and well-rounded individuals through the range of high-quality experiences they offer their pupils.

SOFT SKILLS

The Prince's Trust is a UK charity which has always demonstrated a passionate commitment to the needs of young people, and has been successful in gaining financial support from major commercial institutions such as the HSBC bank. The Trust recently produced a report, "The Prince's Trust Results for Life Report", on what are sometimes referred to as "soft skills". This means those skills that are not taught or measured in the way traditional academic subjects are, but which are nevertheless identified by employers as being very important to success in the workplace – skills such as being a valued team member, being an effective communicator and possessing confidence. The Trust's report found that teachers, employers and young people themselves recognised that soft skills were as important to achieving success in life as good grades.

However, something that is of real concern is that the report found that 43% of young people say their soft skills are not good enough and 46% say their confidence is too low.

> **Carey:** *I'm a bit pessimistic about schools in general. The kids and the teachers seem to be worked to death for the SATs league tables, based on one day's performance – a snapshot.*

ARE (STATE) SCHOOLS DOING ENOUGH TO DEVELOP STUDENTS' SOFT SKILLS?

The Trust's report certainly found that teachers placed importance on developing soft skills. Three of the top five skills which teachers consider the most important for students to develop at school are communication, confidence and teamwork. An amazing 92% of teachers think that supporting students to make progress with their soft skills can help to improve their overall academic performance.

However, more than half the young people who took part in the survey said that although school had helped them with maths and literacy, they didn't feel that school had helped them much in developing soft skills. This is echoed by the fact that more than a quarter of teachers (27%) think that most of the students they teach don't yet have all the soft skills required to do well after school, and 91% think schools should be doing more to help students to develop these skills.

Also, of those already in the workforce, 72% felt they themselves didn't have all the soft skills necessary to do well when they first started working. 50% said that when they started work they lacked confidence, 23% said communication skills were a problem, and 19% said they lacked the ability to look after their mental health. Looking further back, 64% felt a lack of soft skills meant they struggled to find a job when they were starting out. Another study by the EY Foundation and the School to Work Campaign published in September 2017 confirms what employers are saying: 50% of small and medium employers (SMEs) think that young people do not have the core non-technical skills needed. They were concerned about young people's skills in working as part of a team, problem-solving, resilience, the ability to communicate, organisational skills and punctuality.

PRIVATE SCHOOLS KNOW ABOUT SOFT SKILLS

As we saw in the previous chapter, developing these soft skills is already well embedded into the curriculum in independent schools, which is something, again as we have seen, that they are proud to highlight on their websites. Alan Milburn's 2012 report on social mobility says that fee-paying pupils benefit from an emphasis on "soft skills" such as teamwork and communication, which are imparted through sport, music and drama. This makes good sense when you think about it: if you have problems with spelling or maths, you might find it difficult to make really good progress in these subjects. However, if you are a star striker on the football field, chair of the debating society, the best singer in the choir or brilliant at acting, not only will your friends admire you for your talents, you will feel good about yourself – it will increase your confidence. Feeling good and having confidence also seems to help you do better in the areas where you aren't naturally gifted.

In his autobiography, *So, Anyway*, the comic actor and writer John Cleese mentions that his friends from the grammar school felt less confident than those who had attended public schools: "Most public school boys had a confidence that they felt they lacked, and so, in social situations, they often felt ill at ease. They wondered how the public school chaps had acquired their sense of self-assurance and I certainly couldn't tell them."

> **Stella:** *Listen and support, encourage, always take an interest, praise.*

EMOTIONAL WELLBEING AND CONFIDENCE

Elsewhere in this book I talk a lot about effective communication and the importance of talking with and listening to your child, but in the following sections I focus specifically on how parents can ensure their children develop a healthy mindset and a sense of emotional wellbeing and confidence.

> **Carey:** *If my child seems to be in a bad mood, I tell her that she has a choice about how she can influence how her day goes, by changing her mood.*

So, what do we know about developing children's confidence and self-esteem? What follows isn't supposed to be a comprehensive treatment of research into psychology over the past 50-100 years, but my aim is to give an insight to parents into some key ideas which I believe can have an important impact on children's psychological development and wellbeing. If one of the reasons for parents to pay for private education is to ensure that their child has confidence and high self–esteem, what does this mean? Why does it matter? Let's begin by thinking a bit more about the meaning of self-esteem (or self-belief) and confidence.

SELF-BELIEF AND CONFIDENCE

Roedean, one of the UK's most well-known independent schools, describes one of the school's main aims for its pupils thus: "[to] develop a sense of self-belief and the confidence to embrace aspirational goals and realise that they are attainable".

The dictionary definition of "confidence" is "a feeling of self-assurance arising from an appreciation of one's own abilities or qualities". Psychologists, on the other hand, have usually examined self-esteem from the negative perspective, by focusing on the problem of low self-esteem. The child with low self-esteem has a sense of herself being of low or little value. High self-esteem brings to a child a sense of being important to the other people in her life or to the world. So, where do self-esteem and confidence come from?

DO WE INHERIT OUR PERSONALITIES?

There is some evidence that psychology – the way we think and reason, together with our emotions and feelings – is affected at least in part by our genetic heritage. Some conditions which affect our thinking and learning have been shown to run in families, e.g. schizophrenia, some forms of autism and dyslexia. Most of us who have had more than one child (including me) believe that children have innate differences from birth.

However unique they seem to be when they are first born, what children experience, especially in the early years, makes a big difference to how we grow and develop, and how successful we are in our school life, work and relationships. Many studies have shown that our life experience and family relationships have a very powerful impact on how we think and develop as human beings.

> **Flora:** *I've had five children and all five were completely different from birth.*
>
> **Isabel:** *Babies aren't blank slates when they are born. But you influence them – you're their first teachers.*
>
> **Nigel:** *My two girls are like chalk and cheese, although they have some similarities, maybe through genetic or parenting influences.*
>
> **Elaine** (a mother of five): *They already have their personality, even newborns, and respond differently according to their interests and preferences.*

EARLY BAD EXPERIENCES DON'T HAVE TO HOLD YOU BACK

For example, most people have heard of post-traumatic stress disorder, where a person's thinking, feeling and general wellbeing are affected by a stressful event such as involvement in a catastrophe or war experience. This can seriously affect their ability to behave normally or lead a happy existence. Perhaps this could mean that children who have suffered family difficulties, abuse or traumatic experiences in their early life could be significantly affected, and some of the effects might influence the whole of the rest of their lives. However, I don't believe that a difficult start means you can't make a success of your life. Many successful people had a less than perfect early childhood (for example, Oprah Winfrey the TV star, Maria Dan Gracas Silva Foster, head of the oil giant Petrobras, and Thomas S. Monaghan, the founder of Domino's Pizza). On an everyday basis, every teacher has known children who are delightful, hardworking and making excellent progress **in spite of** a difficult start in life (including some from refugee families).

As parents, the more we find out about what helps children to learn and be happy, the more we can nurture them to become successful human beings who fulfil their potential.

> **Maggie:** *I've never seen the point of giving children a hard time unnecessarily.*

I believe that there are three particularly significant areas of psychology which have critical impact on the psychological development and emotional wellbeing of children: Attachment theory, Conditioning and Positive Thinking.

ATTACHMENT

In 1951, John Bowlby, a psychologist who was interested in the development of maladjusted children and the experiences of those who had been neglected, carried out a ground-breaking study of children who had experienced difficult circumstances such as being separated from their parents for a period of time. As a result of his research, he developed a detailed theory about the importance to small children of "attachment". By this he meant that to develop socially and emotionally, young children need the close involvement of an adult figure, who becomes trusted by the child, who treats her with **care, respect and closeness**.

Many children who show behaviour problems have had difficulties with attachment in their early years and need particular help to overcome this.

This is particularly true of children who have been in the care of the local authority because of Child Protection concerns (perhaps involving neglect or abuse). Experts in early childhood care and education, such as nursery teachers and nannies, have a very detailed understanding of the importance of a child's mental and emotional development and so make sure the children in their care feel more secure by relating to them in a warm, gentle way with lots of praise and encouragement; they avoid upsetting or frightening small children with shouting or punishments.

Children who find settling into school life difficult, or who show difficult behaviour, need special attention. Nurture Groups exist in schools to support students with barriers to learning arising from social, emotional or behavioural difficulties; and a recent Nurture Group Network (NGN) survey of 100 NGN-accredited nurture groups noted that "the majority of children [in nurture groups] have experienced significant trauma such as separation from family, exposure to family conflict, abuse, divorce, a new home or school, illness and hospitalisation, death of a loved one, parental drug exposure and maternal depression – 19% of primary school students in primary school nurture groups and 42% in secondary school have a diagnosed psychiatric disorder, most commonly ADHD" (Pilot Study Summary published on the NGN website).

Nurture Groups were created by Marjorie Boxall, an educational psychologist, to help children improve their behaviour and wellbeing by creating a calm, positive and gentle but firm atmosphere, attempting to replace damaging early experiences to provide the child with a sense of security and positive self-esteem. Boxall's system led to the creation of a range of Nurture Groups in schools across the UK, and has transformed the school and family experiences of thousands of children who might otherwise have been excluded because of their behaviour problems. Key aspects of this effective practice have been a high staff to pupil ratio and close involvement between staff and parents, which has often involved a kind of "coaching" in parenting skills. Unfortunately, recent cuts in education funding have resulted in the closure of much of this excellent provision.

GENTLE AND KIND

This shows us that the types of relationships we develop with our children are very important to develop **confidence, wellbeing and contentment**. Being gentle and kind is a very important part of making a child feel happy and content. If your own parents seemed very harsh and "disciplinarian", it can be very difficult to avoid being the same with your own children. You might feel that this is how parenting should be; but if you can adapt your parenting to be loving, gentle, encouraging and interested, the rewards are immense – not just for your child, but for you too. Please note, being loving and kind is not the same as saying, "Do what thou wilt shall be the whole of the law" or taking an "anything goes" attitude to rules and boundaries. This can lead to real problems (as explored further in the next chapter).

> **Elaine:** *I had a challenging, stilted childhood, not at all loving. I had no encouragement, no love at home. I used to wish I could live in a children's home. This has influenced me majorly – I have done the complete opposite. I decided, "I will support my kids. I will tell them I love them and am proud of them. I will find out their passion and encourage them." I told them not to be afraid to be different and to pursue their dreams. I have put parenting at the centre of my life.*

CONDITIONING

B. F. Skinner and other behavioural psychologists more than 50 years ago conducted a series of experiments on animals to test theories about how behaviour could be changed by the responses to it. He found that rewarding desired behaviour (which he called reinforcement) was an effective way of encouraging the behaviour desired (in animals and in people). The simplest form of reinforcement is praise: "Well done!"

Skinner also found that punishment (e.g. shouting or even smacking) for unwanted behaviour did help to discourage it, but was not as effective as encouraging the behaviour you do want. These theories have had a significant influence on behaviour management in schools: children whose behaviour needs to improve are often helped by a programme which gives rewards for good behaviour (sometimes referred to as a Behaviour Support Plan). The same principles are used by parents who are effective at managing their child's behaviour, and by celebrity "Supernanny" Jo Frost, who has made a number of TV programmes helping families to develop calmer and more positive family relationships.

POSITIVE THINKING AND OPTIMISM

Interestingly enough, much of this way of thinking is reflected in the more recent focus on positive thinking which has been gaining popularity over the last 20 to 30 years. The American professor Martin Seligman, sometimes called the "guru of optimism", has shown that people with positive attitudes are not only more successful and less likely to suffer stress-related illness, but are also likely to live longer.

OPTIMISTS LIVE LONGER

In the USA in 2009, a study following the health and wellbeing of women aged 50 and older (led by Hilary Tindle, Assistant Professor of Medicine in the Pitt School of Medicine's Division of Internal Medicine) found that over an eight-year-period, optimists were **less likely to die** from all causes than pessimists, including being 30% less likely to die from coronary heart disease. People were classed as optimists and pessimists based on a definition of "optimism" as the expectation that good, rather than bad, things will happen.

Martin Seligman is often described as the "father of positive psychology", and his work, together with other similar psychological research, is the basis for a range of personal development and training courses often undertaken by high-flying executives with the intention of becoming more effective in their work roles (see Steven Covey, mentioned below).

POSITIVE PSYCHOLOGY AND MEDICAL TREATMENT

In recent years Cognitive Behavioural Therapy (CBT) has come to be widely accepted as a very effective treatment for depression – a Department of Health study published in 2001 showed it to be more effective than medication alone. CBT is based on the same principles of positive psychology as coaching and executive programmes like "Investment in Excellence" from the Pacific Institute.

Some of the main messages to participants in CBT are:

- Be **positive rather than negative** – concentrate on happy and optimistic thoughts, not negative and pessimistic ones

- **Believe in yourself** – believe you can achieve what you want in life – adopt a "can-do" attitude

- Life is not a matter of luck or chance – **you** are in the driving seat of your life

- Focus on the **future**, not the past

- Have a vision for how you would like your life to be and set **goals and aspirations** for yourself

POSITIVE THINKING IN BUSINESS

Steven Covey's *The 7 Habits of Highly Successful People*, which is aimed at aspiring executives and managers, includes many of these ideas, but well before him, many thinkers and writers expressed the importance of how thinking affects success and the impact of a sense of self-belief. Napoleon Hill wrote a very successful book called *Think and Grow Rich* and Norman Vincent Peale wrote another widely read book, *The Power of Positive Thinking*.

However, more than 100 years ago a French pharmacist and psychologist, Emile Couhé, was really the **original** father of positive psychology. He was based in Brittany, France and began treating patients with all sorts of illnesses, including depression. He believed in the power of the mind (self-hypnotism) to overcome many physical and psychological health problems. Couhé believed that people should have in the front of their consciousness: **"Every day, in every way, I'm getting better and better."**

Also, the enormously successful car manufacturer Henry Ford once said, **"Whether you think you can or think you can't, you're probably right"** (think about it!)

The idea that how we think influences what happens to us and how people respond to us is reflected in much effective practice in coaching and other types of support designed to help people manage their lives, overcome challenges and be happy and contented.

WHY THIS KNOWLEDGE IS IMPORTANT FOR THE FUTURE OF OUR CHILDREN

In the UK, there have been reports recently about rising rates of depression and even self-harm in our children. Praveetha Patalay at the University of Liverpool produced a report in September 2017 of research she had led on depression rates in teenagers. Alarmingly, it showed that there has been a dramatic rise in the number of 14-year-olds showing worryingly high rates of depression – in the case of girls, it was 24% of the cohort in the study. This compared to a similar study carried out ten years previously which showed 12% of girls showing the same signs. The proportion had **doubled in ten years**.

Karen Sullivan, a psychologist and child care writer, writes in *Sec Ed* (a magazine for secondary education professionals) about the **rising rates of self-harm** in adolescents in the UK. Apparently, girls are more at risk than boys (girls under 18 needing hospital treatment for self-poisoning increased from 9,741 in 2006 to 13,853 in 2016, and in the same period those admitted for cutting themselves quadrupled from 600 to 2,311 cases). This concern is not unique to the UK – the pressure on teenagers to achieve academic success in India has led to rising rates of suicide (8,934 in 2015).

The situation isn't helped by some of the dark sites on the internet which promote and encourage self-harm, and in a strange way make it seem somehow exotic and attractive.

Why do some young people self-harm? Some victims describe cutting as a coping mechanism, which if they have a sense of numbness or feeling of being disconnected from their community or school, confirms to them that they are still alive. Bullying can obviously cause children to self-harm or even commit suicide, and schools have a duty of care in this respect – to have good systems through their safeguarding responsibilities to deal with bullying effectively.

BE ALERT

It is really important for parents to be **alert to signs of depression** which could lead to self-harm, even though navigating the choppy waters of adolescence (with its determined bids for more freedom and independence) makes parenting very challenging at times, and even harder to communicate well with your child. Hertfordshire University has carried out a series of studies in this area and say that **early prevention** of self-harm is key. They say that good quality Personal, Social and Health Education (PSHE) in school is very helpful by providing opportunities to discuss feelings of despair which may lead to self-harm and depression. It also enables the school to embed an atmosphere of support for all pupils and also encourages them to look out for each other, alerting staff if necessary when they are really worried about one of their classmates.

SEAL AND PSHE IN SCHOOLS

PSHE, as we have just seen, stands for Personal, Social and Health Education. SEAL stands for Social and Emotional Aspects of Learning, and is a nationally recommended programme for schools published by the government in 2005. Schools have made some progress in these areas since that date, and SEAL is a very well-constructed programme, designed to be used in assemblies and in class time. It uses stories and pictures to help children deal with the many challenges relating to relationships and feelings, and includes a theme called "Good to be Me" which aims to encourage children to focus on the **positive** aspects of their lives. It begins the task of consciously trying to teach children to think in ways that help them become happier and more successful. In India, as a result of the pressure on teenagers and high suicide rates, Manish Sisodia, the Delhi Education Minister, has introduced classes on how to be happy.

Another factor which has had impact has been the requirement for all schools to have measures in place to record and deal with incidents of **bullying**. When schools are inspected, a great deal of emphasis is placed on their policy and practice of "safeguarding". This aspect of the school's work includes Health and Safety, Child Protection and Bullying Policy and how well it is managed.

WHY SHOULD WE SUPPORT OUR CHILDREN IN LEARNING THE SKILLS OF POSITIVE THINKING?

We live in an age when many adults are seeking to develop their own thinking to help them become more successful and happy. Learning the skills of positive thinking gives people a huge advantage and helps them to fulfil their potential – so shouldn't it be a **priority for parenting** and within our education system?

Maggie: *When teaching, I tell the children, "In my room, you come to have a good time."*

Apart from the obvious value of encouraging children to feel happier and preventing depression and self-harm, we need to think of the changes in our economy and employment opportunities. The fastest growing form of employment is self-employment. The level of self-employment in the UK increased from 3.8 million in 2008 to 4.6 million in 2015 (ONS, 2015). This is the highest number of self-employed people since comparable records began in 1992 (Government statistics).

SELF-EMPLOYMENT

Self-employment involves selling one's skills and time to other people. The significance of this change in the UK today is being recognised by the huge range of networking opportunities – Chambers of Commerce and local councils running networking breakfasts, business organisations which provide networking opportunities such as Business Networking International and 4Networking. There are also powerful and successful web-based social networking sites such as LinkedIn, Facebook and Twitter. It is really important for self-employed people to have high levels of **self-confidence** and **self-belief**. The important point is this: **good social/communication skills and confidence** are key to presenting a successful image to potential clients, especially in face-to-face networking.

WHAT THIS MEANS FOR PARENTS

Positive feedback and confidence

- To help your child to develop positive skills in communication and self-confidence, your contacts with your child should be in the ratio of at least 9:1 **in favour of the positive.** It is extremely powerful to see how your child's confidence grows and flowers when you do this – if you don't believe me, just try it!

- If you and your partner have got into the habit of being over-negative (which is extremely common, especially if this is how your parents were and/or you have more than one child, a number of stresses and a busy life), try to watch out for each other and encourage one another in the direction of providing more positive than negative feedback to your children, ideally in the ratio recommended above.

- When your child is doing something which you would like to encourage, **actively** notice and praise her, e.g. if your child is sitting quietly reading a book, "It's good to see you concentrating on that book and sitting quietly. Well done," or if your child brings a toy to her little brother, "That is a very kind thing to do. You are a good big sister!"

- Other positive things you can drop in are little comments like:

  o "I really liked the drawing you did for me at school yesterday."

  o "I am really pleased to see you sitting nicely at the table. Well done."

  o "I do love to hear you sing – maybe you will be a famous singer!"

  o "My goodness, you have done well to keep your clothes clean today; that's good."

o "You are walking very sensibly and holding my hand. Well done."

> **Maggie:** *I believe in giving children "golden coins" – telling them what they are good at or have done well in so that they can keep good feelings about themselves.*

Given the concerns about depression and self-harm in adolescents already mentioned, trying to help them to focus on the positive aspects of their lives and achievements is very important as it **improves their emotional wellbeing**. Remind them of their successes and strengths – yes, they may well curl their lip and snap at you in return... it's part of the joys of parenting that age group! You could suggest taking them to a show or football match you know they are interested in, to give them the opportunity to enjoy themselves and maybe open up about any worries. It's helpful to encourage them to spend time with friends who help them relax and feel good, or maybe other relatives they are close to, and remember that the school should be able to provide advice and support if you are worried about the possibility of self-harm, as should your GP.

WHY SHOULD I? (THE ANSWER IS: BECAUSE IT WORKS!)

A few parents I have suggested this strategy to have said something like, "Why should I praise her for doing that? She should be doing it anyway!" This is particularly likely if their own parents rarely praised or encouraged them. The answer is simple: **because it works!** If you want more good behaviour and high self-esteem, and a calm and happy family atmosphere, praise your child for doing what you want her to do. In psychological terms, you are **reinforcing** the behaviour you want and giving your child a sense of being valued and liked. How can that be a bad thing? If you find the idea of doing this a bit difficult, just try it for a week and see the effects it has on family life and relationships.

SHY?

Some parents worry that their child is underconfident or too shy. Identifying a way for a child to excel and feel success can make a big difference – it might be dance, music or drama classes, sport, art or joinery. It is a good idea to be alert to anything your child shows a talent for so that you can nurture it and use it as a means of developing confidence and celebrating success. This might mean joining clubs or classes, or spending time with your child in the activity, or seeking out friends and relatives who can help develop the skill or talent. Whatever it is, make sure you are **interested** in what she is doing, praise the child for her achievements and talk about her positively to others when the child can hear you, e.g. "Hey, why don't you sing Granny the new song you learned at your singing club?"

GOAL SETTING AND SHAPING DESTINY

Encourage your child to have a vision for what she wants to achieve in life – talk about this to her and try to help her to build a clear picture of what success will look like and what the path to success will involve. Set goals for your child and praise her for meeting them. At the same time, **discourage the idea that life is a matter of luck or chance** – talk to your child about what she can do to make her dreams become reality so that you promote the sense of her control over her destiny. Lou Tice, of the Pacific Institute, aptly calls this sense of personal control and responsibility "self-efficacy".

WHAT THIS MEANS FOR PARENTS

Here is an example: if your child goes to dancing school or football club, she may harbour a passion to dance at Sadlers' Wells or play for Manchester United (although these ambitions are likely to change as she grows). It is best if you don't tell your child what she has to do to reach her ambition, but ask her open questions (i.e. those which can't be answered "Yes" or "No") to help her work out her goals for herself. In this way you help your child to practise the thinking she needs to become more self-determining – this is a **skill that lasts for life**.

For the young dancer it could go like this:

(After a trip to see a West End ballet show or a film with dance like *Billy Elliot*)

"I would like to do that."

"What would you need to do to be able to dance on the stage in London?"

"I would need to be a really good dancer."

"How will you know if you're a really good dancer?"

"Everyone will clap me really hard when we have a show at dance classes."

"Is there anything else?"

"When I have my next exam, I will get a high grade."

"What would be a high grade?"

"More than 90%."

"How can you make sure you get more than 90%?"

"I will practise my dancing every day."

"Well done. I think you have made a plan!"

This is goal-setting, which helps to shape the child's thinking in a positive way. It assumes that the child's future success is in her own hands. This same idea is included in every manual or development course promising business and career success. This sort of discussion also relates to the value of Philosophy for Children, which we'll discuss later in Chapter 6 "Language, learning and thinking".

LIFE'S GOALS AND AMBITIONS CHANGE

Of course, you need to realise that your child's vision for the future will change and adapt as she gains more experience and finds out more about what her possibilities and potential are. The nine-year-old may want to become a ballet dancer; the same child at twelve might want to be a lawyer, at fourteen, a doctor and at seventeen a pop star! The important thing is to constantly encourage and nourish the child's view that **she can control her future**, rather than life being a matter of luck or fate.

Chapter 4

BEHAVIOUR, WHY IT MATTERS AND HOW TO MANAGE IT

This chapter is about children's behaviour, why it is important, and some suggestions on how to make sure your child is not disadvantaged by poor behaviour.

There is a huge range of opinions about the rights and wrongs of behaviour, and most children progress to adulthood without any serious problems, although there can be occasional testing times. The press and the media (TV, Facebook and YouTube, especially) often feature problems with children's behaviour. Most of us have witnessed behaviour by children which might be considered naughty or bad, which might include tantrums, destroying their own or others' possessions, hitting others and refusal to do what parents tell them. It has been shown that a common reason for teachers leaving the profession is poor behaviour by children, especially where this is condoned or backed up by parents (The Response of the National Union of Teachers to the House of Commons' Education and Skills Committee Inquiry into Secondary Education Teacher Retention, June 2012).

EXCLUSION

Most parents are aware of what is meant by the term "exclusion". It is the legal term for what used to be called "expulsion" in schools: children being required to leave the school and not being allowed to return, either for a set period, perhaps a week or two, or permanently.

HOW MANY CHILDREN GET EXCLUDED?

One in 20 secondary students will experience at least one fixed-term exclusion each year. Two-thirds of fixed-period exclusions in secondary schools were given to pupils who had already received at least one earlier in the year. Research by the children's charity Barnardo's found that any exclusion places some young people at risk of getting involved in antisocial behaviour or crime. The risks associated with permanent exclusion, which affects about one in 500 secondary school pupils (0.17%), are even greater.

Children who have poor behaviour (often described as EBD, Emotional and Behavioural Difficulties) are significantly disadvantaged within the education system and in adult life. For obvious reasons, they are much more likely to be permanently excluded from school. If permanently excluded from school, they are much more likely to be involved in law-breaking and imprisonment and are less likely to achieve a good standard of education. A study carried out by the IPPR (Institute for Public Policy Research) in Scotland found that of the 86,000-strong prison population in the UK more than 54,000 had been excluded at school.

BAD BEHAVIOUR CAN AFFECT YOUR LIFE

Further evidence of the lifelong impact of behaviour problems is gained from data about children placed in Alternative Provision (AP) or Pupil Referral Units (PRUs) – both terms are used for the schools and residential centres for children excluded from mainstream schools. Large numbers of pupils in AP do not achieve decent qualifications. In the year 2011/12 only 1.3% of pupils in AP achieved five or more GCSEs at grade A* to C or equivalent including English and mathematics – this compares very badly to the rate in mainstream education, which for the same year was 59.4%.

So why does all this matter? Because problems with behaviour, the main cause of exclusion, cause serious difficulties with achievement at school. Even when children are placed in small group settings where they get a much larger share of the teacher's attention (most PRUs have a much smaller pupil to teacher ratio than the average private school!), they don't generally achieve well.

LOW QUALIFICATIONS = LOW PAY

Not doing well in exams is, unsurprisingly, associated with high unemployment and low-paid work. The online Careers site www.allaboutcareers.com says that graduates earn on average **£9.17 per hour more** than those who don't have qualifications.

The point of all this is that poor or unacceptable behaviour significantly disadvantages some children – not only does it result in poor exam results, it affects how much you earn later on. It can have a lifelong effect. At one extreme end of the spectrum, just a lack of awareness of expected manners (saying "please" and "thank you", not interrupting when others are speaking, using bad language) can disadvantage a young adult trying to get a job. Where these social rules are not understood, it can make senior staff or other people in power reject a young person or not give her the right kind of attention and encouragement she needs. This kind of disadvantage has already been mentioned in terms of the current focus on "soft skills". So, swearing, aggressive behaviour and physical violence can all lead to exclusion from school, general disapproval and even arrest and/or imprisonment.

PARENTS AND BEHAVIOUR

The other important point to make is behaviour problems make life very difficult for parents and other family members, so it makes sense to have a plan about managing it. I have seen parents who were on the verge of a nervous breakdown because of their child's behaviour. (I have also seen parents very tired and stressed by their attempts to bend over backwards to meet their demanding child's wishes and expectations!)

So, parents have a very important role as regards behaviour in a number of ways. Parents are the first teachers a child has to give her an understanding of behaviour which will help her get on in life. Children need **boundaries** to feel secure and to provide them with guidance on how to be "in the right". If you are allowed to follow every impulse without considering any rules and do whatever you like, how can you make the choices which will help you in the future? Also, **is real life like that**? Can you decide not to follow laws and regulations and still get on in life OK? I would suggest that, although a brief period of rebellion in the teenage years is normal, **you can't**.

WHAT THIS MEANS FOR PARENTS

Developing good behaviour in children – Positive feedback

As already mentioned, the most effective teachers and parents use positive feedback as a very powerful tool. As adults relating to children, one of the mistakes we commonly make is to only notice children when they are doing something you would prefer they didn't! If a baby is cuddled and picked up if she screams, she quickly learns that if she screams, she is picked up – she has "trained" her parents! The parents' response has reinforced the screaming. I'm not saying you should leave a baby to scream if she is distressed – there's a great deal of advice and commentary out there about whether you should or shouldn't – I am just emphasising that if you always react in the way the baby wants, you are training her to do it again.

Likewise, a toddler who is ignored unless she screams or hits out is likely to continue with this bad behaviour because it is the one that gets results for her. Children crave attention, and for them negative attention (being shouted at or told off, for example) is preferable to being ignored.

> **Helen:** *I felt every time she cried I had done something wrong.*

WHY NURSERY STAFF ARE BRILLIANT

By contrast, if you give your child positive attention and praise if she does what you want, this is the most effective way of shaping her behaviour. Smiling and saying, "good girl/boy" when they do the right things is what works well when your child is very young. When I was first involved in the education of nursery age children, the calmness, gentleness and patience of the teachers and nursery nurses was astonishing to me. They have a really tough job with, perhaps, twenty-five three-year-olds to deal with who have (up to that moment) had a large amount of attention from one special adult (normally Mum). Getting them to co-operate together as a group is incredibly hard. **I couldn't do it**. Nursery staff achieve this by constantly praising the behaviour they want: "What beautiful sitting, Chloe," "Eyes on me, well done," etc.

Being positive and encouraging is not just for small children, however. It works with all ages (and also with adults!) Actively notice and find something to **praise your child** for as much as possible.

> **Ken:** *For confidence, music is a wonderful skill to give to children. It stays with them forever.*

If you are not used to the idea of praising your child for doing what you want to shape her behaviour, I appreciate that it can be hard to consciously change the way you respond to your children. This is especially true if your own parents were a bit negative and controlling with you, but it is absolutely critical to your child developing good behaviour and positive self-esteem. It might also reduce your stress!

You can of course influence children by behaving as if it is inevitable that they are going to do well in any situation. This can be very powerful – you are making it clear that you expect them to do well, and usually they will rise to your expectation.

> **Maggie:** *When children come into my lesson with a report sheet to record whether they've been good or not, I always say, "I'll sign it now. I know you will have a good lesson with me." Then they relax and it's "in the bag" already.*

All this is not to say that negative feedback isn't sometimes needed (just that the ratio of positive feedback to negative feedback should, as suggested in the previous chapter, be very heavily in favour of positive).

IS HITTING YOUR CHILD ALWAYS WRONG?

> **Philippe:** *I once hit my small son on his bottom and saw my handprint on it. I never did it again. This was behaviour that was learnt from my parents. I didn't know how else to manage the situation.*

This is a difficult and controversial question, on which the debate continues to this day. Certainly, it is illegal for publicly employed teachers or nursery staff to smack someone else's child, but the law in most of the UK does allow a parent to smack her own child if and only if this amounts to "reasonable chastisement and does not leave a serious mark".

Some parents think a child should never be smacked. I remember years ago talking with a friend who had two small boys. We had a chat about whether you should smack them if they were naughty. She was quite shocked at the idea and said quite firmly something like, "That's a terrible thing. Adults shouldn't be able to hurt a child whatever the circumstances, just because they are physically bigger. It's quite, quite wrong."

In October 2017, the Scottish parliament decided that the law should be changed so that this defence for parents is removed, which means that the law could be different in Scotland from the rest of the UK. Sally Holland, the children's commissioner for Wales, expressed her disappointment that a legal defence for hitting children still existed throughout the UK. Some other high-profile figures, such as former Children's Commissioner for England Maggie Atkinson have argued for an outright legal ban on smacking. Others argue that mild smacking on an occasional basis when really warranted is justified.

Whilst obviously not wanting to condone violence against children, I do recall vividly two occasions from each of my two daughters' early years. On the first, I was standing at a bus stop in London when my tiny daughter (aged about two) just suddenly ran across the road. (I think she saw something – a little dog, perhaps). Luckily no cars came along at that moment. I dashed after her to the other side of the road with my heart in my mouth and slapped her bottom. I didn't think about my action – it was based on pure adrenaline.

> **Helen:** *I learnt from my parents to smack a child to make them do something. I felt bad about it, and I did smack the older two, but tried not to as they got older.*

The other occasion was with my younger daughter when she was less than a year old. As soon as she became mobile, she kept heading for plug sockets to try and insert her fingers or toys into them. On several occasions, I distracted her, but she was a very strong-willed little girl and kept determinedly returning to the plug sockets. So, I gave her a stern look and said, "No!" in a fierce, loud voice. Whereas with my older child this would have resulted in instant obedience and maybe even a few tears, this little charmer looked me straight in the face and stuck her hand against the plug socket again. So – and I'm not proud of this – I slapped her hand. She cried, but after that avoided the plug sockets. The lesson had been learned: those things cause hurt – it's best to stay away.

TANTRUMS – THE "TERRIBLE TWOS"

> **Deborah:** *I think with tantrums you just have to let her do it and stay calm. I have found it difficult when she bites me in frustration, so I tell her off.*

Almost all children go through a stage from around the age of two when they develop a desire to go their own way. It is as if your child suddenly realises that if they don't do what you say, the sky won't fall in! This is sometimes called the "terrible twos" and it can be a stressful time for parents. It's not uncommon to be in a shopping centre or large supermarket and hear the outraged screams of a small child who doesn't agree with her parent's decision to remove from her the large bar of chocolate she has just taken off the shelves.

> **Karen**: *Why don't people help you when they see your little child having a meltdown?*

INDEPENDENCE AND FRUSTRATION

Tantrums are caused by frustration as the little one tries to be more independent and take more control of her world – unfortunately the world doesn't always co-operate! It's particularly difficult because children of this age haven't yet learned enough language to explain what's making them angry or what they want. This also makes it difficult for you to reason with your child and talk her through the situation to calm her down (which is much easier when she is a few years older).

> **Helen A:** *I was surprised when my son started to have extreme tantrums at the age of nine months. We then found it was connected to his tonsillitis.*

WHAT TO DO

For the parent it can be tricky and stressful, but first just remember **YOU** are the adult, so **you have to stay calm**. Parents know their own child best, so you can usually learn to recognise the signs of a tantrum brewing and spot the sort of situation which might result in a tantrum (e.g. it's towards the end of a long hot day, with signs of a snuffly cold and not enough sleep the night before). When she kicks off, sometimes you can calm your child by distraction – playing a favourite tune or cartoon on your smartphone or pointing out the dog walking outside. If that doesn't work, it's best to ignore the tantrum (as long as she can't hurt herself in her rage), but be ready with a cuddle and a kind word of praise **the instant** she starts to calm down.

DON'T WORRY ABOUT ASKING ADVICE

Something that can be really annoying is when your child behaves perfectly with someone else (their minder, say) and never has tantrums. If so, don't be afraid or embarrassed to ask the person: "I'm glad my little girl never gets into a strop with you. Can you give me a hint on how you manage that?"

> **Richard:** *My daughter does show stubbornness. As a teacher, I know behaviour management techniques, but she still doesn't always respond – so I resort to bribery.*

In most children, tantrums usually stop by the age of four or five, when you can reason with your child and talk through how she is feeling. So, your life calms down for a few years… then…

THE OTHER MAIN TRICKY PATCH – ADOLESCENT HORMONES

When your child reaches puberty, and starts making the journey into adulthood, there are hormones surging around her body. Hormones affect your feelings and mood (know any women with pre-menstrual tension?) So, hormone changes can result in moodiness, bad temper and unpredictability. You might wonder why you always feel like you are walking on eggshells around her. You may be thinking where you have gone wrong in your parenting for your delightful co-operative child to suddenly turn into an angry, sullen or depressed adolescent.

It isn't your fault! It's what my mother (having been through this as a parent **five times**) calls "that horrible age". In a way it is like the terrible twos because your child wants more independence, and is trying to establish her own identity and preferences. As with the terrible twos, you need to remain calm and in control. You need to be strong and not put up with unacceptable behaviour (for example, hitting you or other family members, smashing furniture or windows) at the same time as making sure your child knows you love her and want to help.

> **Isabel:** *I felt reasonably in control even during adolescence. I don't know why they didn't have tantrums. I used to hold my breath until I was unconscious as a means of trying to control, but I grew out of it!*

WHAT TO DO

First, choose your battles. Does it really matter if she has black fingernails and inch-thick makeup at the weekends? This is part of developing her own identity. There's nothing to stop you making gentle comments like, "Oh, you're going to apply for that Saturday job at the posh spa up the road… not sure if they'll like the eight piercings in your face, six big rips in your dirty jeans and the dreadlocks, but why not have a go?"

The same applies to the state of her bedroom. If it's **her** bedroom, and she's happy for it to be a mess, just keep the door closed. (Obviously if she shares it, or rodents move in, it might be different!)

HAVING A BIG ROW

If an argument seems to be getting out of control or really nasty, remember **you're the adult** so **you** have to manage the situation! Say, as calmly as possible, something like, "I think we're both too het up to continue with this. I'm walking away so we can sort it out later when we both feel better." This gives her a bit of space to calm down; maybe she is feeling a bit overwhelmed by her own strong feelings of anger and frustration.

> **Isabel:** *The most difficult thing for me was letting go because I was afraid for them. It was difficult allowing them to become adults e.g. going to clubs etc. I gave lots of advice about sticking with your friends and don't let one go off on their own.*

It can be tempting to give in to, say, an angry demand to stay out all night at a party at a friend's house, just to keep the peace. But not only will this result in a sleepless night for you, you will have taught your child that kicking up a big fuss is a guaranteed way of getting her own way! This won't make life easier in the future...

> **Russell:** *One of my daughters has quite recently matured and suddenly doesn't need to be helped with the right versus wrong – she knows automatically. I can see how she is changing into a different person.*

> **John:** *Our eldest daughter had serious disabilities, so it took a great deal of our time and effort to manage her. I think this affected our next daughter who started being quite naughty when she was at school. When she was at secondary school she didn't like it, so we sent her to another school where she could be a bit more of a free spirit. I'm not sure this was right because it started her downhill into not conforming. She had a very violent stage where she kicked doors in and slammed them. As a result, at about 17 or 18 she had a flat to live in with others who had the same interests. We had a very unsettling seven years.*

CAN GRAN HELP?

You may have relatives or friends who can help by letting your child go to see them (grans can be good for this) giving your child (and you) a breathing space. When she is calm, try to have a low-key chat about whatever caused the shouting match to see if it can be resolved. Note this is **not a telling off**, but an opportunity to close off the situation. Be brave and state your feelings clearly, e.g. "I'm so glad we're OK now. I have this rule about where you stay and who with because I love you and want you to be safe."

SOME SERIOUS SITUATIONS WHERE YOU NEED HELP

If your child's behaviour seems to be getting seriously challenging (hitting you and/or other family members) or you have worries about any of the following:

- depression/suicidal thoughts/eating disorders

- serious friendship problems

- bullying, including cyberbullying

- the sexual relationships she is developing

- drugs or alcohol abuse

- criminal activity

…it is wise to seek help. You can approach your child's school for help and advice or maybe your GP.

There is also some excellent guidance to be found on the internet, although it needs to be carefully chosen (for example, there are some sites which promote a particular religious perspective which may not be relevant to you).

The Family Lives site at www.familylives.org.uk and the Relate site at www.relate.org.uk are both particularly clear and helpful. The Family Lives site provides online discussion where parents can share the problems they are dealing with, and Relate provides online counselling sessions with a trained adviser free of charge.

Another very useful site is Young Minds at www.youngminds.org.uk, which tackles many common worries parents have about emotional wellbeing and mental health as well as an A-Z list of challenges and where you can find help.

> **Alice:** *We had a difficult time around the age of 15/16 to 18. You are so close to them, but they are so vulnerable. Some of my daughter's friendship group have experienced self-harm, depression and, in the wider circle, anorexia. When this happens close to home it makes you less complacent – you cannot take anything for granted. One of my daughters lost weight when she was in the sixth form. You can't control it – you can only guide and support, but not control.*

EVERYDAY GOOD PRACTICE FOR BEHAVIOUR – GUIDELINES AND RULES

Why do you need guidelines and rules? You need them to give a shape to how you respond to behaviour. You need to try to give your child an idea of "how we do things around here". As a parent, you can't just make it up as you go along!

Have a few clear and simple guidelines or rules which **everyone** in the family keeps to (including parents – or you will hear that familiar cry "That's not fair!") It is best to agree these in a family discussion and express them in a positive rather than a negative way, because it is much easier for the subconscious brain to process and respond to a positive instruction than a negative one. This means removing the sense of "don't" and substituting "do". It can be really challenging to change the way you express these rules, especially if it is different from what you have experienced as a child from your own parents. This means you have to make a real and conscious effort to think about the best way to do this. It is not just about "pasting in" new knowledge; it's about unpicking old experiences and habits, which is much harder.

Here are some examples showing the difference between rules expressed in a negative and a positive way:

Negative	Positive
We are not nasty to each other	We are kind to each other
We don't shout at each other	We talk calmly and politely to each other
We don't hit people	We are gentle and nice to each other
We don't throw food	We eat our food sensibly and neatly
We don't swear	We only use nice language
We don't go off with friends	We always tell Mum or Dad where we are
We don't make a mess in the bedroom	We keep our bedrooms clean and tidy

You might want to think for a few minutes about how you want your child's behaviour to change and how you will express this with a positive, rather than a negative, emphasis. What does she do that drives you crazy? Now think about this carefully and frame an instruction or comment which is **positive**. The more you do this, the easier the habit will become.

> **Lesley:** *I didn't understand why they did what you didn't want them to after you had given them reasons not to. Being a parent is not the same as being a friend. My eldest son, now an adult, has said, "I am glad you kept me disciplined so I didn't go off the rails."*

Having rules, or boundaries, gives you a framework to explain why you would like to see some behaviour change, e.g. "Jack, you took away your brother's train and made him cry. In this family we are kind to each other. Was that a kind thing to do?"

WHAT YOU CHOOSE TO DO, NOT WHO YOU ARE

When discussing behaviour, it's important to always focus on the behaviour, not the person. For example, never say, "You are a bad girl," but instead say, "That wasn't a kind thing to do." This is because it is very difficult for a child to cope with the idea of herself as a person being condemned. From the child's point of view, if it is **me** that is the problem, I feel stressed, powerless and anxious – it is **me, my identity,** under threat.

YOU CHOOSE YOUR BEHAVIOUR

It is much more effective to express concern **about the behaviour**, which you as an individual own – you are responsible for it, you control it, and you can choose to change it. This helps a child to feel powerful and in control (recall that in the previous chapter we discussed the importance of a child believing she is in charge of her own future), especially if positive changes in behaviour are commented on in an encouraging way.

Always focus on the idea of **choosing** behaviour when your child has done something she shouldn't have done, because you are teaching your child that she makes choices, rather than her behaviour being outside her control. When a child has learned enough vocabulary (by the age of around three), it is a good idea to have a little discussion routine which embeds this idea when you deal with incidents.

A conversation about a problem

Instead of saying, "You naughty, stupid girl! Why did you throw that plate on the floor and break it?", try something like the following:

"Why did you do that? Who is in charge of your behaviour?"

"You are, Mum."

"No, I'm not. I didn't decide that you should throw that plate on the floor. Who is in charge of your behaviour?"

"My teacher? The government? The police?"

"Did your teacher, or the government or the police decide you should throw that plate on the floor?"

"No… I suppose not…"

"So, who is in charge of your behaviour?"

"…I am, Mum."

"That's right. So why did you **choose** to throw that plate on the floor and break it?"

From the child's perspective, there is no easy way of avoiding responsibility for her own actions after this sort of conversation. As an additional benefit, by following this process, you are further enhancing the child's understanding that she has **power and control over her future and destiny**.

CONSEQUENCES

It is important to have clear and reasonable consequences in response to keeping to or breaking rules, relevant to the child's age, and build in a warning stage. Saying, "Stop screaming or I will take away all your toys for a week," is over the top for a three-year old. However, saying, "You are a good boy and are sitting at the table nicely today, much better than yesterday, so tonight we will ring Granny and tell her that," gives a powerful message that this is the behaviour you want to encourage. You have also "doubled-up" the positive feedback (from you and also from Granny), making it even more effective.

This strategy also relates back to actively noticing and praising your child for doing what you **want**, instead of getting cross or angry if they do something you don't want.

A WARNING

A quick warning: never, ever threaten anything that you can't or won't follow through on, or the child will not believe you or trust what you say afterwards – you are shooting yourself in the foot! Sometimes, parents who are frustrated when their child doesn't do what they want, decide to "up the ante" and threaten ever more dire consequences, but this can be risky. A threat such as "You took your brother's sweets, so I will ring the police and you will go to jail," or "I've told you before. Tidy up your room or you will have no Christmas or birthday presents for two years," is pointless in terms of trying to improve behaviour. You can't realistically follow through on these sorts of sanctions. And after that, why should your child believe what you say in the future?

STICK TOGETHER

As parents, it's really important to agree the family rules and consequences before trying to apply them. You need to have a clear discussion together early on in your career as parents about what really matters, because families are unique and what is important in one family may be seen very differently in another. For example, let's say one of your family rules is going to be that you don't interrupt when other people are speaking; this will only work if **both** parents subscribe to it. If one of you always allows a small child to interrupt adults who are speaking (i.e. that parent breaks off the conversation with another person as soon as their child speaks to them), that is what she will learn to do. (And because there is a good reason for making the rule in the first place, in some situations this will disadvantage her. If a teacher has 30 children in her class who all believe they can interrupt at will, this can lead to a chaotic situation!)

Also, in terms of "soft skills", as adults, we have strong social codes about interrupting another speaker, and children need to learn this when they are small so that it becomes a positive habit which doesn't cause them problems when they grow up.

Not every family will value the same things in equal measure, though, so it is important that you as a family have a clear discussion and decide what guidelines and rules really matter to you.

BE CONSISTENT (EVEN IF MUM AND DAD AREN'T TOGETHER)

> **Darren:** *It can be tricky to agree discipline between parents to get consistency. The child knows how to play parents off against each other.*

A clearly agreed rule means that the child is not put in situations which are difficult to understand – "I can interrupt Mummy, but Daddy will shout at me if I do." It's also important to always back each other up. Children are experts at playing one adult off against another. "But Daddy says I can…" may produce a temporary warm glow that your child loves you, and some parents get in a situation where, because of a lack of agreement or clarity, they compete for their child's affection by applying different expectations. This can be particularly difficult if parents are no longer together as a couple, but even in this case it is still very important to agree guidelines and rules between you and apply them as consistently as possible, if nevertheless independently. This is for the benefit of the child's wellbeing and future development. I have seen a number of children confused and distressed by parents giving them different messages about what is acceptable, and some of them needed special help (including counselling) to overcome behaviour problems in and out of school.

SPECIAL EDUCATIONAL NEEDS

All of what I have written above applies to the vast majority of children. However, some children are born with, or develop, conditions which mean these strategies might need to be supplemented or supplanted with specialist advice. For example, some children have a form of mild autism known as Asperger's Syndrome, which means they see the world and other people in a very particular way, and parents can need specialist advice on how best to help them with behaviour issues. Other children have conditions such as Attention Deficit Disorder or Hyperactivity, which makes it difficult for them to sit calmly and concentrate for any length of time. Sometimes this is related to diet or allergies. If your child is not yet at school, you can get advice from your local GP or health centre, and there are very useful support groups for parents which can help with advice or guidance. If your child is of school age, your child's teachers will almost certainly notice these sorts of conditions and you will need to meet with the school's Special Educational Needs Co-ordinator who will know where to get specialist support and advice.

DON'T LOOK FOR A LABEL

A word of warning about this, however. Check that you are not looking for a label to give your child, when she doesn't really need one, but you just need to adapt your behaviour management style. Rely on professional advice and assessment – if you decide to give your child a label after looking it up on the internet, there is a risk that you will just be giving her a reason to NOT take responsibility for her behaviour. ("It's not her fault, she has Asperger's/ ADHD.") However, most specialists will in any case provide advice based on the suggestions above, even if your child is assessed as having a particular condition.

IT'S ALL ABOUT BEING POSITIVE

As also mentioned in the previous chapter, on self-esteem and positive thinking, the key to ensuring children show behaviour which sets them on the path to success is to focus always on the positive – expressing rules **positively rather than negatively** and making sure that you actively notice and praise what your child does right, rather than telling her off when she does something you don't like or don't approve of.

Chapter 5
LANGUAGE, LEARNING AND THINKING

YOU THINK IN WORDS

Have you ever thought about **how you think**? Most of us think in a mixture of words, images and feelings. Pick a topic – anything at all which you feel strongly about… now try and think about it without using words. Difficult, isn't it? **You need words to think**, especially about anything complicated or challenging. So, developing your child's language skills is one of the most important ways you can help her learn and develop her thinking skills.

GROWING LANGUAGE DIFFICULTIES

In the UK we have a crisis of language difficulties – not affecting those children who are learning English as a Second Language as you might think, but from those native speakers whose first language is English. Most teachers have witnessed a child's frustration at being able to understand a concept or idea, but not having the vocabulary to express it. There is also no doubt that many children with behaviour problems – particularly boys – have difficulties expressing themselves in words, something which is very frustrating for them. The government's

Better Communication Research Programme, reporting in 2012, showed that the number of children with speech difficulties had leapt 70% in six years. It estimated that as many as 1.2 million youngsters now struggle with speech. Half of pupils in some areas start school **unable to put sentences together**. This is very worrying.

COMPUTERS, TV, MOBILES

> **Peter:** *Every new device that comes along can cause problems because it changes your lifestyle. Entertainment is more individual now – you can all be in the same room and all be looking at something completely different. I think people do adjust to these new things.*

In the modern age, we are surrounded by electronic media which transmit information and images 24/7. Technology is all around us, supporting a huge range of business and personal activities, and most of us as adults find it difficult to cope if we can't get reliable access to the internet!

> **Alex:** *I use the internet to look up anything I need to know to help my child. The knowledge of the whole world is at your fingertips.*

It is pretty amazing to think we can converse quite easily with people on the other side of the planet (using Skype or FaceTime); we can do business with the whole world – and the world is our oyster. I have a gadget (which I am sure will be considered "old hat" within a few years) called

Alexa, and I can tell it to find me a radio station, play music by my favourite singers, tell me about the weather tomorrow or find out what time the local supermarket closes tonight. Fifty years ago, my father was working in the early days of computers and he travelled to Australia to install a new computer for a company there – it filled ten storeys. By contrast, many people now have smartphones which have far more capabilities in a little gadget which fits in one hand.

> **Nigel:** *IT definitely helps me personally – it's great to have a computer with the spellchecker and have information on the device. Also, we gave our girls mobiles so that we could know where they were.*

WHAT'S WORRYING ABOUT TECHNOLOGY?

Although computers, the internet, mobile phones and TV allow information to be transmitted quickly and easily, the way that we allow them to dominate our lives and the way we allow children to spend a great deal of time using them brings us a new set of problems and concerns, especially from a learning point of view.

TV is essentially one-way communication. The TV lets the watcher be passive; it tells you things without requiring you to respond, interact or show your understanding. The LENA Research Foundation study, which we'll discuss in more detail below, notes that "The more television time in a child's day, the lower his or her language ability scores tended to be."

Computers, the internet and mobile phones do allow two-way communication, of course, but a great deal of what is required is in low-level, undemanding language, maybe just single words.

Unsupervised access to the internet can also mean children are subjected to images of violence and pornography, which can be very damaging. Every school's Child Protection Officer can quote examples of children who have been affected by these. (In fact, if a child is being exposed to this sort of material, it can be seen in law as a form of emotional abuse.)

> **Darren:** *Our children are too young for social media. My young son seems to be slightly addicted to IT, and I think it can cause problems with social skills if they become dependent.*

Unsupervised access to the internet, especially social media, can result in children being bullied online and this causes serious emotional distress – see below about cyberbullying.

A more recent report from The Legatum Institute (2018) linked the rise in anxiety, self-harm and other mental illness with high social media use by young people, and recommended that the UK follow Iceland's strategy (introduced in the 1990s) which encouraged parents to spend more time interacting with their children. This initiative saw a dramatic reduction between 1997 and 2007 in the numbers of young people who had been drunk or had smoked marijuana or cigarettes.

Sue Palmer's book *Toxic Childhood* describes the impact of modern technology on our children much better than I can in this chapter, including the way some children (especially boys) can seem obsessive about or hypnotised by the lure of mobiles and computer games machines. Is it a coincidence that boys have higher rates of dyslexia, autism and speech and language difficulties than girls? Are the gadgets all around us actually damaging our ability to communicate?

SMARTPHONES IN SCHOOL

The Daily Mirror (online edition 11th September 2017) recently reported on research by Nominet (the company which manages the domain names ending in .uk) about the use of smartphones. Secondary teachers said that they lose the equivalent of 11 days a year in teaching time due to disruption caused by smartphone use. 27% of them witnessed social media cyberbullying, and 17% had seen pupils sharing explicit or porn images. Teachers feel that the use of smartphones results in pupils achieving a lower grade at GCSE than they could have done, and it has been pointed out that if you see something disturbing, you can't then "unsee" it. And in much the same way, if you decide to share something on social media which you later regret, you can't then "unshare" it (even if you or the platform delete it, others will have seen, and perhaps saved, it). As *The New York Times* memorably put it the internet "means the end of forgetting" with one's online past being difficult if not impossible to erase. People today are leaving an online record of their lives like never before, with friends, potential employers and enemies alike perhaps just a mouse click away from forgotten and regrettable photographs, videos or posts.

CYBERBULLYING

What is cyberbullying? It can involve sending nasty messages and pictures about or to a person. We have all heard about Twitter being used to make really unpleasant attacks on and threats to politicians and others who are in the public eye. It does seem that young people, who are often the quickest to pick up the skills of new technology, are experiencing some really difficult and unhappy times with the use of technology for bullying – there are even apps which disguise the identity of the bully.

A survey of 10,000 young Britons in July 2017 revealed that the worst social network for cyberbullying is Instagram. 42% of those who had been cyberbullied had experienced it through this site. Of course, the internet makes it easier for bullying to take place as it is much easier to post something unpleasant online than to actually go up to another person physically and say the same thing to their face. (Many female MPs and other women in prominent positions have faced very unpleasant threats and harassment online via Twitter from people who doubtless wouldn't dare make such attacks if they couldn't hide behind the anonymity of the internet.)

Carey: *I'm not very worried about cyberbullying, because I don't intend for my daughter to have any social media contacts until she's at least 13-14. Even then, I will only allow it if I can oversee it. My nine-year-old has a mobile phone, but the deal is she only has it if I'm allowed to check it.*

The Children's Commissioner for England, Anne Longfield, is clear that parents need to be aware of their children's use of the internet and the risks, especially as some studies have linked social media use to depression and low self-esteem. An American professor (Jean Twenge from San Diego State University) carried out some research on 1.1 million children and found that those who used social media and the internet the most were **twice as likely** to be depressed or anxious. Some children – even as young as the age of nine – can become quite obsessed by social media, even checking their phones during the night when they should be asleep.

> **Flora:** *They don't socialise or play as they should and maybe they get information they shouldn't know...*

Unexpectedly, while communication has never been easier with anyone else in the world, in the UK (and some other countries) we have seen that at the same time as the use of technology has increased, children's ability to **use language** has declined.

SPEECH AND LANGUAGE AND ACHIEVEMENT

The National Association of Head Teachers published the results of a survey in September 2017 which showed that more and more children are arriving for their first year at school **not ready to learn** and benefit from education:

> *Respondents identified a number of issues that mean that some children are not ready for school, in particular concern about their speech, language and communication skills were highlighted. The*

social, emotional and physical development of some children were also cited as areas of concern.

HOW MANY WORDS?

"The more parents talk with their child from birth, to age three, the more likely their child will excel academically later in life. And that sets the stage for other successes in the child's future.

If a parent only talks a little bit, the conversation is only about business. 'Stop that.' 'Get down from there.' 'Come here.' But when a parent advances the conversation beyond business, the topics automatically change. The words used in conversation change, too. And that makes all the difference later in the child's intellectual life."

(Todd Risley, later Emeritus Professor of Psychology, University of Kansas)

The importance of language and vocabulary to learning has been proved in more than one study. Todd Risley and Betty Hart in the US demonstrated that the **number of words** a child hears has a clear impact on their academic performance in school. They studied the link between the number of words a child heard between the ages of birth and three, and their intelligence test scores, and produced a groundbreaking report in 1995. The results were astonishing: a child who heard 7,430 words a day was likely to have an IQ of 79, whereas a child who heard 21,105 words a day scored an IQ of at least 117. They also found that the **variety** of words spoken had an impact on the child's IQ. The study is often referred to as "Thirty Million Words" as this was the difference in the number of words heard between children in middle class/professional families and those in disadvantaged families, including those dependent on benefits.

A similar study was undertaken a few years later but using new technology called the LENA System (Language Environment Analysis System) which is a gadget which was "the world's first automatic system for measuring key elements of children's language learning environments". Basically, it is a small piece of technology about the size of a mobile phone which is worn by the child in the pocket of a sort of tabard. It records all the words a child uses or hears and the number of conversations she takes part in. This technology made it much easier to systematically gather information about the language which young children are exposed to. It is then analysed using specialist software. In their report published in 2009, the LENA Foundation conclusions were the same as the landmark 1995 Hart and Risley study: the **number and range of words** a child is exposed to between the ages of birth and three has an effect on how well they do academically at school (and in later life).

THE WINDOW OF OPPORTUNITY

Children seem to have a **window of opportunity** when their language develops very fast. When children receive little adult attention when they are at the early stages of understanding language they fail to develop language appropriate to their age. You may have read or heard about this happening in countries where orphanages are poorly staffed. They can also develop other forms of disordered behaviour such as rocking or making odd noises. There have even been some cases of children who did not have the opportunities to learn human language through their parents – feral children, or those who suffered serious neglect. In the 1960s, Eric Lenneberg developed the theory that it is rarely possible for children to develop language normally after this window of opportunity has passed, in spite of intensive therapy and support.

> **Russell:** *You need to talk with them regularly. Card games, the chessboard and board games help to develop thinking and problem-solving skills and help them socially. We played Cluedo and Monopoly too.*

ASPERGER SYNDROME

A further aspect of communication difficulties is the rise in diagnosis of Asperger Syndrome, which is a disorder related to autism (mentioned previously in the chapter on behaviour). Children with this condition may have difficulty understanding other people's views and need special help to learn social codes and develop social relationships. They also may need support with learning to communicate effectively – this is not just a difficulty with language. Boys are much more likely to be affected by the condition than girls. Research led by Professor Terry

Brugha of the University of Leicester published in 2009 found that 1.8% of men and boys in England had a diagnosis of autism, compared to 0.2% of women and girls. The ratio of those who use the National Autistic Society's (NAS) adult services was approximately 3:1 in favour of men, and in those that use NAS schools it is approximately 5:1.

Lorna Wing, a well-known expert on autism, in her paper discussing the gender balance in early childhood autism, identified that among people with "high-functioning autism" or Asperger Syndrome there were as many as 15 times as many men and boys as women and girls. (Recently, however, it has been suggested that the difference can be explained by girls learning to hide the symptoms of Asperger Syndrome more effectively than boys.)

Think about it — most of us know someone who is a genius with computers, machines or an obscure specialism, but whose communication and/or social difficulties mark them out as a little odd. Many children with Asperger Syndrome cope with everyday life very well, including in school, but others need special coaching in communicating with others so that they can take part in social situations and manage relationships happily.

It's important to note that schools have a much greater awareness of Asperger Syndrome and autism than they used to, and most can call in specialists who are very familiar with the signs and symptoms. They offer parents help and advice on how to make sure a child gets the right sort of help so she can achieve her best. It's worth remembering that children with the condition feel much safer if there is an established set of rules and routines which they understand and if they are given advance notice of changes to their routine or schedule.

However, the main point for parents when you think about language development is not to worry about whether your child has some sort of Special Educational Needs. It's really about being aware of **the importance of speaking and listening** for children's intellectual (and social) development and thinking of ways to make sure you give them the best support you can. You don't need to be a genius or an expert. **If you can talk, you can help your child do well.**

WAYS OF HELPING LANGUAGE DEVELOPMENT

There are some initiatives which aim to help parents with language development in the early years. In the UK, two NHS paediatric speech and language therapists, Tracey Park and Lisa Houghton, have developed an interactive programme for use in school nursery and playgroup settings which is called "Talking Tots". This involves parents in understanding how to talk with their children in ways that will help develop language skills. By demonstration, group leaders use puppets and other fun equipment to show parents how to use language effectively with their children. For example, nursery rhymes with actions are used to gain children's attention in a fun way. This is a very useful way of learning rhymes and routines to help your child's language development, and you can find out much more about these kinds of activities using the internet, especially YouTube.

If you search for "Nursery Rhymes UK", you will find those videos with the English-UK versions of the rhymes (with those from other countries you might find the words vary from those used in your local Playgroup, e.g. "The Wheels on the Bus"). Most of them have excellent cartoons or drawings with the rhymes, but bear in mind that the most popular ones tend to have lots of advertisements.

In their blog "Talking Is Teaching" published on Huffpost, Maxwell King and Michael Robb make the point that you don't have to spend a lot of money on the latest technology gadgets (claimed to make your child a genius): "Even the poorest parents, unable to afford programs and devices and special educational applications, can harness the power of talking, of creating the language-rich, affirmative environment needed to support young children's prodigious instinct for learning. Just talk… talk, talk, talk… while you are doing the dishes, trimming the bushes, watching a television show… anything and everything in your everyday life. Not only does it make your child feel special, it is also one of the most effective ways that a parent can prepare a child for a lifetime of success."

What really counts, as King and Robb make clear, is that it is so important to spend as much time as possible talking with your child about what is going on in her life and the things that are interesting to her. It's just about being aware of the importance of speaking and listening to children's intellectual (and social) development, and thinking of ways to make sure you give them the best support you can. You don't need to be a genius or an expert. **If you can talk, you can help your child do well.**

> **Peter:** *We always talked; we always ate together in the evenings. Sometimes we would ask them about something which had happened which was good and something they didn't like. This gave some time to reflect, and if there was a problem, you could nip it in the bud.*

INVOLVE OTHER ADULTS

Involving other family members in talking with your child is also very important, because it will be letting them hear a wider range of words and ideas than you and your partner can provide on your own. Maybe Grandad can talk about who is the best player in the football team they support, Auntie Jane can describe her recent trip to Saudi Arabia, Uncle Bob can talk about the new gadget he has fitted to his car, and the nice lady next door can describe how she cuts out and sews clothes. The rich opportunities for people in your circles to help develop your child's language skills are **endless**. Think about the people you know and their knowledge, and you will be amazed at the variety and possibilities: just in my family, the subjects which spring to mind which they know about include aeronautical engineering, promotions and events, the oil industry, pub renovation, dentistry, classic car maintenance and repair, law and order, TV production, sailing, cooking, HGVs, history, Australia, France and New Zealand.

You will almost certainly find that the people in your circles are happy to talk about what they know, and quite flattered if you say, "Could you please have a bit of a chat with Sophie about your hobby of collecting antique pottery? It will help develop her vocabulary and her skills in language." Afterwards, don't forget to ask your child what she found out and what she thought about it, as well as anything she found surprising.

PHILOSOPHY FOR CHILDREN

In the last few years there have been some developments in schools to help children in using language effectively. In the UK, some schools have developed Philosophy for Children (P4C) as part of their curriculum. This has the advantage that children's language and thinking are developed by thinking of questions to ask and taking part in open discussions, listening to each other and taking turns in expressing opinions. Where it has been introduced into schools, Philosophy for Children has shown good evidence that it improves children's attainment. In 2015, Durham University's Education Endowment Foundation reported on their evaluation of the impact of Philosophy for Children in schools and drew the following conclusions: "1. There is evidence that P4C had a positive impact on Key Stage 2 [ages 7-11] attainment. Overall, pupils using the approach made approximately two additional months' progress in reading and maths. 2. Results suggest that P4C had the biggest positive impact on Key Stage 2 results among disadvantaged pupils (those eligible for free school meals)." The same report found that "teachers and pupils generally report improved behaviour and relationships."

WHAT DO YOU MEAN – PHILOSOPHY?

The *Cambridge English Dictionary* gives this definition of philosophy:

"the use of reason in understanding such things as the nature of the real world and existence, the use and limits of knowledge, and the principles of moral judgment:

René Descartes is regarded as the founder of modern philosophy."

I think the word philosophy sounds a bit scary for the average modern parent – as if it is a highbrow activity only for people who work in universities or other well-read adults. Certainly, when I had my daughters, if anyone had suggested to me that I needed to employ the principles of philosophy to help them develop intellectually and socially, I would have thought they were mad!

On the other hand, we can all appreciate that people have different opinions about controversial subjects and we all know that other people can be completely convinced of something we personally don't agree with. A philosophical discussion takes place in an atmosphere of mutual respect, and involves being able to listen to the point of view of others – and even, sometimes, being prepared to change one's own point of view.

Jenny: *My daughter told me, "I don't really like Star Wars – I'm just pretending, to make Daddy happy!"*

GIVE VALUE TO THEIR VIEWS

A key result to bear in mind is that if children are introduced to philosophy, it is a good way of **giving value** to their ideas and views. This is an excellent way of boosting self-esteem and confidence. If you listen to your child's ideas, you are giving the message "What you say is important and worth listening to."

It is enjoyable having in-depth conversations with your children and finding out what they think – they will definitely surprise you sometimes.

> **Richard:** *My little girl is very open-minded. She really makes me think about things –sometimes I think "Where have you got that from?" I have been surprised how she questions things. Sometimes I ask her really silly questions and see her get in a tangle so she can then work her way out. I want her to be inquisitive and to enjoy a challenge, not to see difficulty as something to be avoided*

YOU CAN DO THIS

Having in-depth discussions with your child(ren) is something that all parents can do. Obviously encouraging them to find out about the skills and knowledge of people around them is helpful, as just mentioned. However, it is always a good idea to encourage your child to think of good questions to ask about any event – TV programmes, whatever is currently in the news, family celebrations, visits to other towns and cities and so on. Praise good, thoughtful questions, and be prepared to be astonished at the creative questions your child poses and the interesting angles they perceive things from. Above all, listen carefully to what she has to say and tell her she has good or interesting ideas (even if you don't agree with her!)

Philippe: *Reasoning was something I tried to do – to explain the background, as in history, like the First World War memorials.*

SOME IMPORTANT POINTS ABOUT THE DIFFERENCES BETWEEN BOYS AND GIRLS

I'll be honest, I worry a great deal about the future for the boys in our society (in the UK and the West generally). In all the education settings I've worked in, boys have been significantly overrepresented in a number of worrying ways. They are more likely to arrive at school with speech and language difficulties, have other Special Educational Needs and show attention and behaviour problems, as well as be more likely to have problems related to autism (like Asperger Syndrome, as mentioned above). As they get older, they are less likely to do well at all the key checkpoints, whether it's the phonics test in Year 1 (age 5-6), the Key Stage 1 Assessments (ages 5-7), at Key Stage 2 (ages 8-11) or the GCSE "success markers" at 16.

Boys are more likely to be excluded from school and more likely to get into trouble with the law (sometimes repeatedly). Terrifyingly, they are also more likely to commit suicide. How did we get into this situation and what can we do about it?

BOYS' AND GIRLS' BRAINS

The writer and trainer Geoff Hannan has researched and trained teachers in this area for 30 years and has some clear ideas and recommendations, which are quite controversial in some ways. In recent decades there has been a tendency to assume that gender differences are the result of nurture rather than nature. Boys are usually put in blue clothes from birth, so any adult speaking to them knows they are male; boys are expected to be tough, run around, play football and get grazed knees; they're taught that "boys don't cry"; any boys not fitting into this type of behaviour pattern are described as soft, wimps or "gay". Girls, on the other hand, are expected to wear pink, practise cooking, play with dolls and be interested in hair, clothes and makeup from an early age. And as a result, boys and girls grow up differently.

> **Liz:** *I think the differences between individuals are more important than they are between boys and girls.*

GENDER-NEUTRAL PARENTING

However, many parents of my generation went out of their way to try to make sure their children didn't have gender-specific toys. What is interesting is that, in spite of this, many of them found their children had very clear preferences for different types of toys and play activities aligned to the "traditional" choices. So maybe there is a bit more to it than the different ways we bring up our boys and girls…

BABIES' BRAINS CHANGE

Geoff Hannan draws on research in neuroscience (the scientific study of the nervous system, including the study of the physical aspects of the different parts of the brain and what each controls) to describe how the physical structure of babies' brains changes when they are still in the womb, depending on gender. A male foetus is flooded with testosterone in the early weeks and this seems to affect how the brain develops. By the time they are born, the brains of boys and girls are structured quite differently. What does this mean?

Academics use amazing electrical devices which can be attached to a person's head to show which parts of the brain are active, depending on what is happening at a particular time. One of the main differences in the structure of children's brains is that girls have a thicker connection between the two sides of the brain, the corpus callosum. According to Geoff Hannan and another researcher, David Sousa, this means that girls are better at using the two sides of the brain together for thinking and learning. Sousa also says that the part of the brain which is involved in language is more active in girls. The amygdala (the part of the brain which controls our basic animal instincts) is larger in boys. Some scientists think that this explains why boys are more likely to show aggressive behaviour. On the other hand, the part of the brain which controls memories, the hippocampus, grows more in girls than in boys during adolescence, and this may explain why girls develop better sequencing and language skills, resulting in better performance at GCSE.

BURGERS AT BREAKTIME

In terms of their learning, boys seem to respond better to short-term challenges with fairly immediate rewards. Maggie, a teacher colleague of mine (who is very good at motivating boys), says that the rule with boys is: "Don't promise me a bike at Christmas, promise me a burger at breaktime!"

WHAT THIS MEANS FOR PARENTS

To conclude this chapter, let's answer this question under three headings, "For boys and girls", "For girls" and "For boys", to some extent recapping on some of the important lessons we have learnt so far.

FOR BOYS AND GIRLS

Talk and make your child clever

The most important thing you as a parent can do is to **talk to your child**. This develops vocabulary, but it also develops thinking – because **you need to have the right words in your head** so that you can think.

So:

- Talk to your baby or young child as much as possible. You might not think she understands what you are saying, but this is how she learns and acquires language, and it develops her thinking and social skills.

- Encourage your friends and relatives to talk about their interest and jobs to your child and encourage her to ask interesting questions.

- Repeat nursery rhymes and play simple games involving physical actions ("Incy Wincy Spider", "Round and Round the Garden" and similar, which are accompanied with physical contact with the child and set actions) – there are lots of examples on YouTube! This helps children to understand how language works through rhyme and rhythm. This is a very important early stage in developing communication and is enjoyable for your child.

- **Play with your child** – dressing up, making something, sticking, painting, baking, or playing card or board games – all these provide lots of opportunities to talk and so develop thinking. The other thing about this is that it is fun! As mentioned above, spending time doing something with your child also helps develop her self-esteem. The underlying message to your child is "You are important."

- Use the technique of "**pole-bridging**", which simply means articulating what you are doing in order that the learning is embedded and different parts of the brain are bought into play. This might feel a bit odd at first, but it can be very effective in developing children's understanding and language, and it is an easy habit to get into with your child. It is, after all, just describing what you are doing out loud with your child while you are actually doing it.

An example of **pole-bridging:**

You are baking with your child and you <u>say what you are doing while you do it</u>, and get them to say it too:

"First we are washing our hands to make sure they are clean."

"We are getting the eggs and butter out of the fridge."

"We are getting the flour and sugar out of the cupboard."

"We are measuring the flour to get the right amount. We are weighing the sugar."

"We are cracking the eggs on the side of the bowl."

"We are mixing the butter and sugar together with a whisk."

...and so on

Many early years practitioners working in nurseries use this way of helping children to learn, although they may not call it "pole-bridging". What you are doing is encouraging the child's sense of touch and handling things to link up with their language skills, so that different parts of the brain are working together.

- Put down **your** mobile/tablet, switch off the TV and **have conversations with your child.** It's OK to watch some TV, of course, but try to use it as a conversation starter with your child, using open questions (this means ones that can't be answered with "Yes" or "No").

> "Can you tell me what happened in yesterday's TV show *The Simpsons*? Do you remember who did something very silly? What did they do and why was it silly?"
>
> "What do you think will happen tomorrow? Why do you think this will happen?"

- **Negotiate and discuss** with your children, if you can; don't just tell them what to do. In this way you help them to develop intellectually and socially.

- Recognise that scientific evidence is growing that boys and girls think differently because their **brains develop differently** and help them to overcome any difficulties they might have.

FOR GIRLS

- Help her with deciding to **take action.**

- Make sure she doesn't spend too much time **describing and considering** things before deciding what to do.

- Encourage her to **take risks** and to try things out – "Go on, have a go!"

- Praise taking part in **physically challenging** activities – sailing, tree climbing, the big fairground rides, sports of all kinds.

- Give her opportunities to **experiment and physically handle** and build things including using tools (carefully).

- Make sure Mum and other females help girls to **explore and fix things**, not just with the tidying and cooking!

- Discourage too much analysis and **fretting** about friendship issues.

- Encourage her to read books with strong female characters who take tough decisions.

- Point out successful **role models** of women in traditionally male occupations (like Tammie Jo Shults, the female pilot who successfully prevented a crash when her plane was damaged in 2018, or what about Mary Ellis, the recently deceased RAF female pilot, who ferried over 400 Spitfires and a number of bombers to the front line?)

- Teach her the skills of **assertiveness**, so she can protect her own interests.

FOR BOYS

- Encourage and help him to **explain out loud** what he notices and understands.

- Get him to think of a **range of ideas** and decide how he can choose the best idea.

- Use **challenge**, e.g. "I bet you can't think of five ways to cook an egg in two minutes."

- Praise working with another child and **sharing ideas** and try breaking tasks up into smaller sections with rewards.

- Be a good listener. Ask questions, show interest and encourage boys to explain and go into detail. Praise **talking** about worries at school or with friends and encourage him to think of different ways of dealing with them.

- Encourage him to read stories, **discuss** why characters do what they do and encourage him to predict what might happen next in a story.

- Get him to read instructions for gadgets and games and praise him for suggesting how they could be improved.

- Help him to **plan** – e.g. preparations for a holiday, or how to organise the time he is going to spend on homework, TV and football.

- Think how he uses the computer. Some games can help with planning and decision-making. Show him that the computer can be good for **writing and printing out stories** or documents for special events or games.

- **Be seen reading** yourself, especially if you're male. Encourage other males in the family to be seen reading. Try to build up his reading from his own interests – e.g. moving on from football magazines to biographies of footballers. Let him have comics if he wants (and not just those with the overpriced bit of plastic stuck on the front!)

Nigel: *I got a big buzz out of reading to my kids — it was individual, unstressed time with the child. They remember it and my daughter now expects me to read to her baby — it was "the thing that Dad did".*

Both Mums and Dads should read **to and with** their children — make sure that boys are not left out. **Talk to your sons** as much as to your daughters (whether they want to or not!) and **don't accept** one-word answers.

Chapter 6

DIFFERENT WAYS OF BEING CLEVER

This part of the book deals with some of the ideas and theories which experts – especially psychologists – have produced about intelligence: what it is, how we measure it, and whether it is fixed or can be developed and improved. Some of these ideas are highly controversial and many of them are difficult to prove one way or the other, but obviously most parents want their children to be thought of as "bright".

IS INTELLIGENCE FIXED BEFORE BIRTH?

There are a number of schools of thought about intelligence. Only 50 or so years ago, many highly respected experts believed that intelligence was largely inherited, that it is our genes that decide how clever we are. This provided an explanation for the way people's opportunities to improve their lives (or not) were passed down the generations. "Less able" children were born to "less able" parents.

This is a very sensitive issue, and if this view were correct, it would suggest that there isn't that much that education or quality of parenting can hope to achieve if intelligence is already largely determined at the point of conception. It also means that the quality of parenting we receive doesn't have much effect on our achievement and success in life!

YOUR BRAIN DOESN'T STAY THE SAME

The latest research, however, shows that the brain has more "plasticity" than was previously thought and it continues to absorb information and make new connections throughout life. This explains how people can learn new skills throughout their lives and become better at what they can do. It is why in the 21st century companies see the value and benefits of investing money in teaching and training people to be better at their jobs.

WHAT DIFFERENT PARTS OF THE BRAIN DO

In the last 20 to 30 years there has been an explosion of interest in thinking and learning and there are a number of new theories about how the human brain organises information and how we learn useful skills. Psychologists and sociologists have researched and debated this whole area with great passion and commitment in recent years, and there are many writers who have tried to bring together these ideas and explain them in a way which will help teachers with their job of making the best of children's learning.

NEUROSCIENCE

This work has also been informed by neuroscience, in particular those scientists (neuroscientists) who have studied what different parts of the brain control and described the electrical activity that takes place within them. Such research originated in the study of people with serious brain injuries and what had happened to them as a result of the damage to different parts of the brain. You may have heard of a book called *The Man Who Mistook His Wife for a Hat* by Oliver Sacks, in which he describes people with different brain injuries and how their lives and behaviour were changed. Brain mapping, attributing properties to different parts of the brain, is now a long-established part of neuroscience, and is today informed by sophisticated imaging techniques, which simply put can scan the brain and show what happens during different activities and feelings (and which areas, so to speak, "light up" with electrical activity).

In the remainder of this chapter I will describe just two of the main ideas about intelligence and the influence they have had on what is currently believed about how children think and learn.

HOW ARE YOU CLEVER?

The first of these ideas may well be familiar to some parents as there have been a number of books, TV programmes and newspaper articles about it. In 1983 the American psychologist Howard Gardner started a revolution in our understanding of how people think and learn. He published a book called *Frames of Mind* which was about what he called "Multiple Intelligences". The basic message of this was that not everyone learns and thinks in the same way, and that different types of intelligence result in a wide variation between the skills and aptitudes of different people.

Most people have a perception about what they tend to be good at, or not good at, and this has a powerful influence on their self-esteem and the sort of choices they make in their academic progress and their career choices. For example, you might be thinking, "I'm really good at sport, but I'm rubbish at spelling," or "I can write really well, but I can't draw for toffee."

Gardner's work has had a powerful influence on the thinking of educationalists over the last 30 years. He didn't just make the set of intelligences up in a random way; he had a set of strict rules which had to be followed if an area of intelligence was to be featured in his list. The list included:

Linguistic intelligence: having strong skills with words and language, so being good at reading, extracting information and making speeches.

Logical-mathematical intelligence: being able to work out complex mathematical ideas which follow set rules and see patterns which enable the solving of problems.

Spatial intelligence: the ability to understand, create and manipulate spatial images.

Musical intelligence: the ability to understand, create and remember different patterns in sound.

Naturalistic intelligence: the ability to understand and relate to plants, flowers and animals and weather patterns effectively.

Bodily-kinaesthetic intelligence: the ability to use one's own body with precision and excellence.

Interpersonal intelligence: the skill in being able to understand and recognise the emotions and motivations of other individuals and groups of people.

Intrapersonal intelligence: the ability to understand and reflect on one's own motivation and emotions.

You can almost certainly think of people you know personally or have heard about who fit into one of these categories. For example, a brilliant architect or graphic designer might fit the description for spatial intelligence; someone who is a very effective leader in an organisation could be expected to have strong interpersonal intelligence; sports stars who are paid millions of pounds or win gold medals at the Olympics could be suggested to have bodily-kinaesthetic intelligence.

It is important to note that Gardner never claimed that any person was likely to mainly have strengths in just one of the intelligences. His view was that most people have a **mix of intelligences** with some being much stronger than others. For example, you may know of someone who is a genius at writing long complex documents for parliament (showing linguistic intelligence) and also can play the piano very skilfully, but who has no skills or perhaps little interest in bodily-kinaesthetic intelligence (e.g. sport or dancing) and finds managing their own money very challenging.

"MULTIPLE INTELLIGENCES" MAKES SENSE

One of the main attractions of Gardner's theory is that it seems to make sense from what most of us notice about the people around us. We all know people who are intelligent in some ways, but less so in others. Also, this theory seems to be healthy for how people feel about themselves (or their children). Instead of feeling "stupid" or "dumb" because you didn't pass many exams at school, you can recognise what you **are** good at and feel good about it. It could be argued that our society is going to be much healthier if most people feel confident in at least some areas of skills and knowledge. Maybe this would make people less likely to be depressed. We should also note how our opinions of other people are shaped by what we experience of their particular skills and talents.

> **Philippe:** *When I coached rugby in an excellent state school in Scotland, other teachers expressed astonishment when I mentioned the names of some of my players. They would say things like, "He's a really bad student and he's rubbish at maths." It was amazing how differently they viewed some of my most successful and effective rugby players.*

HOW GARDNER'S WORK HAS BEEN USED IN SCHOOLS AND FOR TRAINING

Since Gardner published his theory, a number of writers and consultants have developed ways to help analyse the sort of thinker or learner an individual is, often using quizzes or exercises which aim to help people identify what their preferred learning styles are. Some of this work in the UK has taken place through the University of the First Age.

> **Darren:** *I'm happy for my daughter to do as much as she wants like drama, ballet, cheerleading, fencing – I wouldn't hold her back from anything.*

From a learning point of view, these ideas have been summarised into the three main "learning styles" of Visual, Auditory and Kinaesthetic. These obviously do not exactly mirror Gardner's eight intelligences but simplify and summarise them. In many schools, teachers have been trained to present lessons in ways which make sure these main learning styles are addressed with the intention that all the children in a class can relate to the main points being taught and can understand them. This idea has also been used to help develop training and development strategies for adults in the workplace.

VISUAL

Visual thinkers learn best from pictures and graphics. They often show a strong sense of colour and are good at drawing, painting, design etc. Visual thinkers might develop as artists, of course, but they could also become fashion designers, architects, interior designers or graphic designers. They are likely to have clear preferences for certain clothes and often their homes are very attractively furnished with a great deal of thought having gone into exactly what kind of furniture and decor they choose. You may know someone whose spelling is terrible or who can't cope with any kind of maths, but who can draw and paint beautifully.

AUDITORY

Auditory thinkers are good with words and what they hear. They tend to enjoy and be good at reading, writing and talking. Sometimes they also have musical skills or enjoy listening to music. Many teachers are auditory thinkers – they tend to enjoy talking and have a wide vocabulary (qualifying as a teacher in the first place means you have been able to listen to a lot of lectures and write a lot of essays). However, as a broad generalisation, secondary teachers tend to be more auditory in style. They can present learning through giving talks or lectures and providing notes. By contrast, it isn't uncommon for primary school classrooms to be a riot of stimulating colours with charts and children's artwork and other things they have created on their walls. This makes some secondary schools look somewhat less stimulating and colourful by comparison.

YOUNG CHILDREN ARE A TOUGH AUDIENCE

There are quite logical reasons for this. In the early years of education, the teacher cannot just talk or provide notes. (Anyone who has visited a school assembly that includes very young children will have found out that they can be a really tough audience if you just ramble on!) Younger children have a shorter attention span and cannot learn through reading and writing as they have yet to embed those skills, so primary teachers, especially those of the early years, tend to use games and dance, art and craft and play in their teaching. They also tend to adopt a lively or even theatrical style of presentation to engage the children. By doing this they make the learning attractive and interesting to all the children in the class.

Many people who have a preference for auditory learning and thinking styles go into careers requiring them to read and/or draft long documents or put together complex statements or arguments, becoming, for example, solicitors or administrators. Linguists and translators, who are interested in words and their meanings, tend to be auditory thinkers too. Some auditory thinkers get very irritated if there is background noise/chatting when they are trying to focus on listening to, or writing, something. (This includes me!)

KINAESTHETIC

Kinaesthetic thinkers learn best from activities involving physical touch and feelings. They are often described as "good with their hands" and tend to like practical activities

— making things and physical movement. Many have good instincts about shape, space and texture, so may become skilled in woodwork, metalwork, needlework or sculpture. Also, you could say that most successful sports stars such as David Beckham, Jessica Ennis-Hill and Serena Williams are kinaesthetic thinkers — they can control their bodily movements with extraordinary skill, power and grace.

Whilst on holiday in Italy, travelling by coach near Positano and Amalfi we passed along a very narrow, winding clifftop road with many hairpin-type bends. There were many challenges in negotiating other vehicles coming from the opposite directions, the sheer drops into the ocean on the side of the road and the foolhardy motorcyclists who occasionally overtook the coach on a blind bend. What was truly astonishing was that the coach driver calmly negotiated these hazards, which sometimes meant undertaking something like a three-point turn in the middle of a very narrow road. We passengers watched the more alarming manoeuvres with our hearts in our mouths as we frequently passed parked vehicles or those coming from the opposite direction with just a few inches to spare. It was quite evident that the coach driver was extraordinarily skilful and didn't even break a sweat at having to deal with some of the near misses. It looked almost as if the huge, heavy and potentially dangerous piece of machinery with its 45 or so passengers was an extension of his own body, so automatically did he manage the coach. He may not have been able to explain to someone else how he managed the driving successfully — he just did

> it. He automatically made a number of very precise calculations and judgements in his head about angles, distances, clearance, speed and balance without even thinking about it. It could be argued that he is a classic kinaesthetic thinker who also showed many aspects of visual intelligence.

Some kinaesthetic thinkers are strongly affected by their feelings and emotions; so they may respond to challenging or happy situations in an instinctive and even physical way (e.g. jumping up and down with excitement – or consider the way a Premier League football team physically celebrate a goal with jumping up and down, and hugging each other etc.)

HOW GARDNER CHANGED WHAT WE THINK OF AS CLEVER

The most powerful aspect of Gardner's work is how it has challenged our view of what we mean by "clever" or "intelligent". Thirty years ago, "clever" normally meant good at reading, writing and maths. Success was measured in GCSE or "O" levels, "A" levels and a degree, preferably First Class Honours and ideally from Oxford or Cambridge. However, there are many people who are not clever in this way, but are highly intelligent and have become very successful – Sir Richard Branson (well known to be dyslexic) who left school at sixteen with a poor record of academic performance is a classic example. Lord Alan Sugar is another, a very successful businessman, recently estimated to be worth £1.15 billion, whose only academic qualification is one GCSE exam.

WIDE RANGE OF CHANCES TO FEEL CLEVER

As we saw in Chapter 2, an attractive feature of independent schools for parents is that most offer a wide range of opportunities to demonstrate skills in sport, drama etc. This means that there are opportunities to **feel success whatever your thinking/learning style**. Having lots of opportunities to excel is very important for self-esteem and success, which builds confidence, initiative and capacity.

Karen: *I would like to see, instead of the end-of-year report, the nursery sending pictures and informing us about successes.*

CRITICISM OF THE IDEA OF MULTIPLE INTELLIGENCES AND LEARNING STYLES

Some psychologists have rejected the idea of learning styles, arguing that there is no evidence that presenting learning in different styles (especially Visual, Auditory and Kinaesthetic) has any effect on the speed of children's learning or the quality of their understanding.

Such critics of learning styles include Doug Rohrer (University of South Florida) and Harold Pashler (University of California, San Diego) who attempted to find evidence that this approach is more effective than others, without success. This is important because, obviously, if you can't find any proof that something works – i.e. in this case, that children learn more and remember more if you teach in this way – it is difficult to say this is what should be done.

Pashler and colleagues state clearly that it is easy to understand why Gardner's work has been so widely adopted in the theory and practice of education. In their report they write: "Another, very understandable, part of the appeal of the learning-styles idea may reflect the fact that people are concerned that they, and their children, be seen and treated by educators as unique individuals. It is also natural and appealing to think that all people have the potential to learn effectively and easily if only instruction is tailored to their individual learning styles." They say the idea is attractive, but there is no proof that it works.

> **Carey:** *I am an NLP [Neuro-Linguistic Programming] practitioner and I am concerned that schools don't always vary the teaching style to fit children's preferences or abilities.*

Taking this point of view, however, misses the point somewhat. It is impossible for a teacher who has 30 children, each with their own particular set of multiple intelligences, to present a lesson in a unique way for each child. The idea of the Visual/ Auditory/ Kinaesthetic structure adopted by many teachers is that it gives **variety** and **repeats** related learning in different ways, so that children with different mixes of intelligences can access it. The other main consideration is that children learn best when they are engaged, and teaching in different ways promotes engagement.

> **Liz:** *It's great to see when a child's brain suddenly lights up because it's found its niche.*

AN EXAMPLE FROM PAKISTAN

An excellent example of this was a recent, carefully structured joint experiment undertaken in Pakistan by Muammed Khan of the Allama Iqbal Open University (AIOU), Islamabad, and Niaz Muhammad of Information Technology, Peshawar. They and their colleagues reported on a very interesting project relating to this theory in *Academic Research International* (2012). This took two groups of secondary age students who were carefully matched by previous ability and test performance. They were both taught the same content as part of their physics course, but the main difference was that one group was taught in the traditional way (i.e. mainly through lectures and taking notes) and the other had a different form of teaching called Activity Based Learning (ABL). The latter involved students in taking part in practical experiments and "hands on" activities. The results of this were quite striking. The group taught through ABL not only achieved higher results in their exams, they showed higher order skills of analysis and problem-solving in their work. The students in the more successful groups used their kinaesthetic and visual intelligences as well as the auditory ones (listening to lectures, note taking and writing essays or test answers). As with the use of "pole-bridging" mentioned previously (talking while doing something), the more successful method seemed to involve different parts of the brain working together.

> **Su** (primary teacher): *To say that teachers using learning styles is an ineffective approach is rubbish. I think it can give a strong basis on to how to teach a child effectively. I am fluid in my teaching; if one style doesn't work for a child, I find something that will work to get them engaged with their learning.*

IS THE CONCEPT OF MULTIPLE INTELLIGENCES DANGEROUS?

There are two main concerns with the idea of using multiple intelligences when we are considering how children learn:

1. There is a danger that it could remove responsibility from the learner (e.g. "I'm a kinaesthetic learner and the lesson was presented in a way which is incompatible with my thinking style, so it **isn't my fault** that I didn't understand/got a low grade in my test.")

This would, of course, not be a helpful response as there is a great deal of research which shows that **taking personal responsibility**, using effort and application has real impact on success in learning.

2. It has also been suggested that it is dangerous to think that your intelligence is **fixed** in any particular way, as such a belief may make a learner think, "There is no point in trying to achieve in an area like maths because I am a visual thinker and my main skill is in art."

To think about this particular issue, let us look at the ideas of Carol Dweck, whose recent work has proved very influential.

> **Liz:** *Perseverance and practice are absolutely essential. Children start with repetition, which enables them to learn and then get some confidence.*

AN IMPORTANT IDEA ABOUT INTELLIGENCE FROM CAROL DWECK

Carol Dweck, like Howard Gardner, is an American psychologist who has studied what makes for a successful learner for more than 30 years. In 2006 she published the book *Mindset: The New Psychology of Success*. She suggests that people, especially children, approach learning in one of two ways, what she calls the "fixed mindset" or the "growth mindset".

Learners with a **fixed mindset** lose confidence if they make an error or don't do well in a test and experience a sense of hopelessness. They are likely to give up, feel like a failure and find it hard to deal with a challenge they are facing. They may abandon the challenge or try to avoid the problem they need to solve. Those with a **growth mindset**, on the other hand, believe that they are on a learning curve, that they can always improve and that if they make a mistake, it is helpful because they can learn from it.

> **Helen A:** *If he can't do something, he might shout, "I can't!" and have a tantrum. I say, "Let's try and think, and not get upset. Try a different way."*

THE IMPORTANCE OF "NOT YET"

Dweck's fundamental idea is that children's learning should be shaped by never telling them that they have failed, but that they have **not yet** succeeded. This is a very important idea because it promotes the idea of **self-efficacy** (i.e. you control what happens in your life). It also suggests that you are on a journey which will result in success and you should **not give up**. It promotes effort and persistence, and the idea that you can control how clever and successful you are. Dweck has used these ideas to show how even children in less privileged settings can become very successful. She tells children that when they push out of their comfort zone, they are making new and more powerful brain connections which make them smarter.

In one of her studies, Dweck showed that students living in a Native American reservation **moved from performing at the bottom of the maths test scores to the top** in their district in one and a half years by using her ideas. This is powerful evidence for her idea that you should encourage children to be constantly trying to improve their learning and to **never give up**.

> **Liz:** *Motivation is everything. Supervise them, but give them as much freedom as possible so that they can learn and explore. Try not to panic too much – children need to make mistakes so that they can learn from them and not have a sense of defeat.*

10,000 HOURS

The journalist and author Matthew Syed, who was a very successful world-class table tennis player, wrote a book on a similar theme about the importance of effort and endurance. It was called *Bounce* and in it he debunks the idea of "natural talent" and claims that most people can become world-class at a sport or another activity if they have at least **ten thousand hours of practice**. He gives lots of examples of how the right combination of circumstance (e.g. an expert teacher of that subject or skill in the family or school) and commitment to practice results in world-class achievement. He says: "World-class performance comes by striving for a target just out of reach, but with a vivid awareness of how the gap might be breached. Over time, through constant repetition and deep concentration, the gap will disappear, only for a new target to be created, just out of reach once again."

> **Jenny:** *It's important to praise the process, not just the outcome.*

This principle mirrors the idea which Dweck talks about by focusing on "not yet" – i.e. you haven't reached your goal, or the highest level you can, and must continue to work to improve.

> **Helen A:** *Life doesn't fall into your lap – go on and get it done.*

WHAT THIS MEANS FOR PARENTS

Can we use these two ideas, which may be telling us slightly different things, to help our children do their best? I think they can definitely sit together in confident and effective parenting.

- To nurture confidence, you need to think about the areas in which your child shines and use this to encourage her and build her feelings of success. It's definitely a good idea to give her the opportunity to feel success in activities which promote and develop her skills. For example, your child might enjoy football or gymnastics, so take her to clubs which help her make progress.

- Perhaps she enjoys art, in which case you could let her have plenty of opportunities to paint and draw. Maybe take her to art galleries or exhibitions or even have her own art gallery at home which you proudly show to family members and other visitors (thereby boosting self-esteem).

- **Teachers recognise special talent:** most teachers get to know early on in their relationship with a class which children shine in particular areas – who is good at art, making things or sport, for example. It is well worth discussing this with your child's teacher. If your child goes to a club where certificates and medals are awarded, it is a good idea to praise your child and display the awards around the house, and it certainly won't do any harm if your child hears you saying what a brilliant artist (or dancer or inventor etc.) she is to other members of the family and to your friends.

- **Effort and determination:** it's important to encourage your child to try hard and develop skills in as many areas as possible. There are a number of areas of learning where not developing a baseline of skills could be a big disadvantage (such as maths, reading and writing).

- Working hard at something you don't particularly enjoy or feel good at encourages **sticking power and determination**, which are common skills in very successful people in all fields. This helps your child to achieve success in life.

- You can also use the idea of multiple intelligences to help your child succeed in areas she finds difficult. For example, a child who has strong visual intelligence but doesn't enjoy reading and finds it hard to remember key facts from what she has read can be helped by using pictures, diagrams, mind maps or flow charts.

- Another example is the way very effective maths teachers have devised practical resources and exercises which give children who have kinaesthetic or visual intelligence ways of strengthening their maths understanding. An example is the use of Cuisenaire rods, which are a bit like using Lego; another is card games like Snap with Times Tables. These enable children to see the problem they are trying to solve in a less abstract way – being able to see something and physically handle it often leads to a "light bulb" going on.

- **Shape learning with talent:** recognise and celebrate your child's skills and strongest talents and the way she uses her intelligence and try to plan activities which use this to help her succeed. (However, it's not a good idea to encourage your child to expect all learning to be presented in a way which fits her preferred intelligence.)

- Give strong encouragement when your child makes mistakes – say, "Great – you are stretching your brain," and praise her for trying her hardest. Some would say we are all born with certain genes which help us be clever in a particular way – and that isn't in our control. **But we can all choose to try hard.**

Chapter 7
LOOKING AFTER THE BODY – NUTRITION AND EXERCISE

YOU ARE WHAT YOU EAT

An interesting study in 2015 found that, in general, independent school pupils were more interested in and aware of healthy food choices. The joint study by The Litmus Partnership and Leeds University Business School reported that independent school students were much more interested in having **healthy food options** than state school students. Also, independent school students were more satisfied with the healthy options provided by their schools. The study also found that children were influenced by their peers about food choices. In the state school setting, they were much more likely to be influenced to choose familiar fast food like pizza than more nutritious options. But does it matter if some children have a better diet than others? Does it give them any advantages?

WHY IS IT IMPORTANT TO THINK ABOUT WHAT YOU EAT?

One of the most important aspects of ensuring that children can thrive and achieve is through making sure that their food leads to the best possible health and wellbeing. It can also affect the capacity to **think and learn**. A number of studies, including the "Young Lives" project supported by Oxford University, have shown that malnutrition affects the development of the brain with evidence from countries such as Somalia where it is difficult for parents to feed their children a balanced diet. It isn't just that children don't have **enough** food in some countries where there is a lot of poverty, they don't get the **right kind** of food, including the vitamins and minerals which help the brain to develop. There is also evidence that where a mother doesn't have enough to eat, or the right balance of foods, it can affect the development of her unborn baby.

Our diets have changed out of all recognition in the last 50 or 60 years, when back then "fast food" didn't exist. And modern diets have been connected to a rising rate of health problems such as heart disease, obesity and diabetes.

Alice: *I think food issues are important. It's really important to have a balanced diet which reflects your own eating habits. I don't believe in having "children's food" and "adults' food". One of my daughters had a dairy allergy – she fainted after eating a lot of cheese. Our children haven't had lots of fizzy drinks – we've encouraged them to drink water and to have a balanced view of food. It's unsatisfactory if they're not adventurous with food, as it helps them to enjoy life.*

Alex: *It's fortunate that my sons have school meals because that helps them have a balanced diet. If they were allowed to graze on what they wanted, they would just eat yoghurts and crisps all day.*

IF YOU HAVE ENOUGH TO EAT, IT DOESN'T MEAN YOUR FOOD MAKES YOU HEALTHY

Ironically, in the UK and the USA although most families have enough food, there seem to be some serious health issues relating to food which affect our children:

- We have rising rates of obesity, diabetes and colon cancer.

- In the last 30 years, more attention has been paid to previously unknown mental health issues connected to food such as anorexia nervosa and bulimia.

- It has been shown by various studies that certain illnesses are connected to eating certain types of food: for example, eating a lot of processed meat (such as bacon and ham) has been shown to affect the likelihood of developing bowel cancer.

- Eating excessive salt (in crisps and other savoury snacks) results in high blood pressure, heart and kidney disease and even bone thinning later in life. It also makes children thirsty, so they may consume more sweetened drinks.

- Obesity is associated with diabetes and also later in life with physical ill-health such as joint problems.

- It is not just physical effects which concern us. Children who are obese are more likely to have **low self-esteem**, less confidence and are also more likely to be bullied.

UK SCHOOLS CHECK PUPIL WEIGHT

Flora: *Protein is important and vegetables and things with vitamin C. They also need bulk from fresh salad and fruit, so they don't get constipated. It's important not to have too many sweets – when I was a child we only had them once a week.*

Every year, children in the first (Reception) and last year in British primary schools are weighed and measured to track the rates of obesity. Experts have voiced deep unease at the figures and their upward trend. In November 2016, Professor Kevin Fenton, the National Director for Health and Wellbeing at Public Health England, said, "It is deeply worrying that more children are leaving primary school overweight or obese than ever before and levels are increasing."

> **Russell:** *I think it's important to avoid processed foods – crisps etc. – because they are highly flavoured which means it makes normal food taste bland. We deliberately developed our children's palates with herbs and spices. But we mainly kept the sweet stuff for parties. I think the idea of sitting around the table for a meal so you can all talk is important. Our children have seen us cooking and not relying on takeaways. I still find it surprising to hear a child say, "I don't eat salmon," and for them to be given alternatives.*

The number of obese 10- and 11-year-olds is now at its highest since children began being routinely weighed and measured in 2006-07. In that year, 17.5% of Year 6 pupils were found to be in that category. In 2016, it was 19.8%, even higher than the previous record high of 19.2% in 2011-12, and the proportion of children classified as severely obese has risen from 3.17% to 4.07%. Maybe this is because our diets have changed so much. We eat much more refined carbohydrate (pizza, white bread, pasta) and sugar, when what our bodies need (especially children while they are growing) is protein, vitamins, minerals and fibre.

> **Carey:** *White bread and other refined foods are high carbohydrate and not good for you. I try to make sure my children have brown pasta. I limit sugary stuff, including cereals and sweets and even orange juice, which is full of sugar.*

WHY IS FOOD A TRICKY ISSUE?

There are lots of psychological issues connected to food and eating. We all have a particular relationship with food (or drink for that matter) and in our earliest days food is provided by our mothers through breastfeeding, so becomes associated with comfort and love. Parents often feel they need to feed their children to demonstrate their love, and in some societies having overweight children is seen as a sign of good parenting.

Nigel: *It is difficult to deal with food issues because we get a lot of pleasure from eating.*

Another thing to think about is the use we make of the easy availability of ready meals from supermarkets and takeaways. I know in many families time is a pressure, especially when both parents work, but relying on food prepared elsewhere means we lose control over what is in it and how healthy or otherwise it is – how much sugar, salt and preservatives it contains.

Helen A: *I believe it is important to cook from scratch and not use processed food. My son eats a wide variety of foods like mussels, calamari and salmon. He loves to cook and understands about the origins of food. I don't give him Coke because it makes him hyperactive, and he doesn't seem interested in sweets.*

WHY WHAT YOU DRINK IS IMPORTANT

Different studies say our bodies are made up of at least 70% water, and some say that our brains are between 70-75% water. So, water is very important for the operation of the physical body as well as for our thinking and learning. You might be aware that certain drinks affect your ability to think and plan clearly (alcohol, for example!) but have you ever developed a headache on a hot day when you have been walking and running around, and realised that it's because you haven't drunk enough water? (I have.) It's worth remembering that our brains operate due to synapses, which are types of electrical connections between different sorts of cells. And, of course, something which transmits electricity is water.

> **Nigel:** *There used to be a drinking fountain in every school yard.*

WHAT ABOUT TEA, COFFEE AND FIZZY DRINKS?

There have been studies which have claimed that tea and coffee are good for you – in terms of helping you stay alert and/or supporting your immune system. However, they have downsides – both are diuretics (which means they drain water out of you by making you go to the loo more often) and the caffeine in both drinks can make you jittery and tense as well as cause sleeping problems. Also, for at least 20 years serious concerns have been expressed about the effects of drinks which contain large amounts of sugar being a major cause of weight gain and dental decay. One

American 2013 study also found that five-year-old children who drank fizzy drinks were more likely to show aggression and social withdrawal.

BUT ARE SWEETENERS BETTER THAN SUGAR?

Elaine: *I have an issue with aspartame, which I think influences children's behaviour and concentration. With my eldest daughter, when we removed it from her diet her concentration improved.*

Eating or drinking food or drink with artificial sweeteners rather than sugar might seem to address the concerns of weight gain and dental decay, but are such sweeteners really a healthy alternative? Aspartame, one of the most commonly used artificial sweeteners, has been tested for safety many times since its introduction in the 1960s, but controversy still rages about its effect on children. Recent reports have also suggested a connection between artificial sweeteners and strokes in older people. There is also another problem with getting the sweetness from an alternative to sugar – it means our taste buds do not develop in such a way as to reduce our craving for sweetness, so it could be argued that they don't help you get away from the addiction to sweets. Personally, I have a sweet tooth, but I often find ready-made puddings sold in supermarkets are so sweet they are actually unpleasant – you can't taste anything but the sugar, so it overwhelms any other flavour. In the UK, because the government has been convinced by medical research of the health problems connected to consuming too much sugar, taxes on high sugar soft drinks have recently been substantially increased.

> **Darren:** *Children should have healthy foods like vegetables and less sugar and sugary drinks. It's important to limit the sweets. I feel strongly about this because I am diabetic (but I would still believe this if I wasn't). My daughter loves sweet stuff in spite of knowing about the dangers, which is worrying.*

THE POWER OF MARKETING

Like us, our children are subjected to all sorts of very clever marketing techniques. These include adverts using "pester power" to sell products which may not be good for them. This can include witty TV cartoons in the adverts, carefully timed during children's programmes and attaching images of their favourite story and comic characters to yoghurts which have added sugar and artificial flavours.

> **Philippe:** *Information about healthy foods changes all the time and is sometimes contradictory, which can make it difficult for parents to make judgements. My son became addicted to a drink called "Sunny D" mainly because it was very strongly marketed. It was promoted as healthy and natural, but wasn't.*

Even pure orange juice, which for many years had been thought of and promoted as a healthy drink for children, has been shown to damage teeth, and because it is high in carbohydrate may also be a cause of weight gain and diabetes.

The only drinks we know for sure that we need and which are safe and helpful for our bodies are a) human breast milk and b) water (presuming it isn't polluted in any way).

DOES WHAT YOU EAT MAKE YOU BRIGHTER?

So perhaps more familiarity with healthy food choices is another factor influencing the higher attainment of pupils in independent schools?

Helen: *I believe they should have healthy stuff like vegetables and salads, and less in the way of sweets and puddings. This is more difficult when your children are older and have their own money so make their own choices. I think a poorer diet results in not being able to concentrate.*

WHO THINKS FOOD IS IMPORTANT?

Medicinenet.com, an American site with information about health and wellbeing, has content produced by US Board-Certified Physicians and Allied Health Professionals. Their aim is "working together to provide the public with current, comprehensive medical information, written in easy to understand language." On the site it states that: "A healthy, balanced diet is not just good for kids' bodies, it's good for their brains, too. **The right foods can improve brain function, memory, and concentration.** Like the body, the brain absorbs nutrients from the foods we eat, and these ten 'superfoods' … can help children boost their brainpower." The ten superfoods listed are: salmon, eggs, peanut butter, colourful vegetables, wholegrains, oats, milk and yoghurt, berries, lean beef and beans.

> **Isabel:** *Vegetables are important. It can be difficult to get children to eat them, but you can disguise them. It's important for children to experience a variety of food. This does depend on the parents and what they eat e.g. if they don't eat salad, the child won't. My small grandchild eats raw tomatoes, cucumber, peppers, sushi and avocado.*

The nutrition writer and TV personality Patrick Holford has carried out a number of studies designed to show that certain foods result in improved health and more effective learning for children when compared to other types. He is a fan of organic produce and recommends the reduction of sugar and salt consumption. He also suggests that use of foods containing refined carbohydrates like bleached flour should be reduced, and is wary of preservatives which lengthen the shelf life of foods such as cakes and biscuits. He conducted an experiment on Irish TV where he cured some viewers of Type 2 diabetes by **changing their diet**. Holford also recommends taking supplements of oil fish capsules to ensure the growing brain has enough essential fatty acids. This seems to confirm what we all thought of as an "old wives' tale" that eating fish is good for your brain.

ORGANIC V NON-ORGANIC FOOD

Another area of interest as regards food and nutrition is that some researchers suggest choosing food without artificial chemicals and pesticides added – organic food.

They believe that because many of the chemicals added to our food have only been in use for a relatively short time (compared to the length of time humans have been on the planet) it is risky to have them in our food. Maybe it is difficult to be sure of the long-term effects on our bodies and the environment.

> **John:** *A variety of vegetables and fruit is good. I think cheap processed food with chemicals in it and sugar-free fizzy drinks are probably worse for your health; it's better to have the natural sweetness in something like a banana. A lot of the chemicals in our food have not been tested long enough to know whether they are good for our bodies. When I was at school we didn't know anything about anyone having things like ADHD and I think the changes in our food with chemicals have caused a lot of this.*

What is clear is that organic food is not a "fad". According to the Soil Association the UK organic market is now growing year on year and worth £2.09 billion. They also report that total sales of organic increased by 7.1% in 2016 while non-organic sales continued to decline.

IS IT A GOOD IDEA TO CHOOSE ORGANIC?

But what evidence is there that organic food is any better for us and, more particularly, for our children's health? Over the last few years there have been at least two major studies on this particular issue. One, published on 8th October 2015 by an international team of experts led by Professor Carlo Leifert at Newcastle University, has shown that organic crops are up to 60% higher in a number of key antioxidants than conventionally-grown ones. According to the study, the difference between organic and non-organic fruit, vegetables and cereals is equivalent to eating between one to two extra portions of fruit and vegetables a day. It also stated that toxic heavy metals (which are thought to **damage human health**) were lower in organic produce.

The other major study (the largest of its kind) was published by Newcastle University researchers Chris Seal and Gillian Butler in February 2016 and showed that organic meat and milk contain around 50% more beneficial omega-3 fatty acids than conventionally-produced products. Seal and Butler reviewed 1,962 reports on the nutritional value of milk and 67 on the nutritional value of meat. They found notable differences in the fatty acid (omega-3s) composition and the presence of certain important mineral nutrients between organic and non-organic alternatives. Omega-3s have been shown to be associated with a reduction in cardiovascular disease, improved immune function and better neurological development.

It seems that whether we like it or not, **food choices have an impact on health** and wellbeing and so are of significant interest to parents wanting to raise healthy children who can achieve their potential.

WHAT THIS MEANS FOR PARENTS

Nutrition affects growth and development as well as intellectual and thinking skills. Remember that our bodies are having to cope with huge changes in our diet in a very short period of time from an evolutionary perspective. It takes thousands of years for mammals to change physically and adapt to their surroundings, but we have radically changed what we feed ourselves in less than 50 years. Maybe increases in certain types of cancer are a response to this – in the West we have a number of cancers such as colon cancer that aren't experienced in cultures where people eat a less refined, low-sugar diet.

These are the recommendations I would make to parents with regard to nutrition for their children:

- Avoid excess sugar (look at the nutrition listing on the sides of food packs – you will be amazed how much sugar is in some foods which you think of as savoury). Also, fizzy drinks can contain as much as six spoonsful of sugar, and recently there has been concern about fruit juices – which may have been thought of as healthy, but without the fibre of the original fruit, carry similar health risks to purified sugar.

- Avoid excess salt to reduce the risks of damage to kidneys, hearts and bones. If you let your child have savoury snacks, choose low salt versions.

- Make sure your child has a balanced diet with protein, fruit and vegetables and fibre. More and more people are choosing food which is organically produced for health reasons.

- Refined wheat flour (as found in white bread, cereals, biscuits, cakes etc.) has a similar effect in the body to sugar. Wholemeal alternatives are much healthier for children and reduce the risks of diabetes and obesity

167

(partly because fibre fills them up so they eat smaller amounts).

- The evidence regarding the health risks of additives such as artificial sweeteners, colouring and preservatives is still uncertain. We haven't been consuming many of these substances for long enough to have a clear idea of what they do to our bodies.

- If you find it difficult to get your child to eat a balanced diet, think about whether vitamin and mineral supplements might be helpful.

- The best drink for children is water – our bodies comprise 70% water and our systems, especially our brains, need it to function properly.

- It can be helpful to try to actively notice the effects that diet has on your child – some parents can tell when their child has had sugar or additives because of the way her behaviour changes.

- Think about whether you think the higher prices of organic food are a good investment in your child's health, given what the studies are saying and the growing demand for organic produce.

EXERCISE AND FITNESS

Hurtling children

I spent some time writing this book in a tiny village in Aude, France. While I was there, in the middle of August, there was quite a large group of children staying in the village in different houses – mainly visiting relatives. They were a mixture of girls and boys between about six and ten, and as children do, they found their own ways of entertaining themselves. What was quite interesting was that one of the main ways they did this was to hurtle around the centre of the village chasing each other and yelling. It was clear that they were having a great time – I think the games they were playing were the French versions of "tag" and "hide and seek", but sometimes it was just running and yelling for the fun of it (as children do).

They seemed to have loads of energy and on more than one night were zooming around in the dark, until well after 10pm. I happened to notice that **all the children were (unsurprisingly) slender and fit**.

> **Philippe:** *When my son was young, I remember showing a small group of his friends how to climb a tree at a friend's place. I fell from a branch near the top, but luckily wasn't injured. I told the kids I did it to demonstrate how to fall out of a tree safely!*

WHAT ARE THE RECOMMENDATIONS ABOUT EXERCISE?

One of the reasons exercise matters is because, as we have already seen, in Europe and the USA we have a crisis in the form of obesity in adults and children, leading to life-threatening conditions such as diabetes, cancer and heart disease (as well as other problems in the long term). But we didn't know until recently that exercise and fitness also have an **important effect on the development of children's brains.** The World Health Organisation (WHO) has recognised the need to promote fitness and exercise, and says it is a shared responsibility for parents, schools and local communities to try to ensure that all children get enough exercise. "Enough", according to WHO, means a **minimum of 60 minutes a day** of vigorous/aerobic activity. The point is also made that exercise which strengthens muscle and bone should happen at least **three times a week.**

STRONGER HEART, MUSCLES, BONES AND LUNGS

There are a number of benefits to this level of exercise. Obviously, one is that children are less likely to become overweight or obese. But there are other physical effects too: the muscles, skeleton, heart and lungs all become stronger and co-ordination and balance improve. Elwyn Firth at the University of Auckland has found that an adult's bones retain a "memory" of early exercise, and they have better density and better bone mineral content than those who didn't exercise – even if they haven't continued with it as an adult. It also means that those children who did have a lot of exercise are **less susceptible to diseases** such as diabetes and cancer as an adult.

Another researcher, Elise Labonte-LeMoyne (University of Montreal), published a report in 2013 that showed that one of the impacts of the mother taking good levels of exercise while pregnant was that it seemed to help their **baby's brain to develop**. It is thought that the pregnant mother's exercise has a positive effect on the unborn baby because they share a blood system while it is in the womb.

> **Darren:** *One of the most important things any parent can do for their children when they are growing up is to encourage them to exercise. This doesn't mean they have to join a team and get all competitive; it simply means they need to get out and be active. It's so easy these days to sit in front of an iPad or a TV, so that being lazy is almost second nature. Apart from all the obvious health benefits they'll get from exercising, they are more likely to continue to exercise as an adult.*

STRONGER MIND AND BRAIN

Apart from the physical improvements which most people won't find surprising, exercise helps to control anxiety and depression, improves social skills and confidence and also results in higher academic performance. This last one might be a bit of a surprise for many parents. Charles Hillman at the University of Illinois has undertaken research which shows that exercise results in better brain development, especially in the areas of memory (the hippocampus) and the part of the brain involved in committing to purposeful action (the prefrontal cortex). It also improves the flow of blood and oxygen to the brain, which helps to make better connections between brain cells. Gretchen Reynolds in *The New York Times* reported on a study which showed that when children took a walk before doing a maths or reading test, **their scores improved** compared to when they didn't.

> **Nigel:** *My daughter really surprised me with her physical ability in sailing. She could sail a dinghy around the harbour at a very young age. It involves a lot of multi-tasking and she could handle a more powerful boat than I could!*

EXERCISE MAKES YOU BRIGHTER

The clearest evidence for the impact of exercise on your child's ability to learn and develop intellectually comes from the study mentioned above carried out by Charles Hillman at the University of Illinois. He led a programme with eight-to-nine-year-olds in a state school. (This age was chosen because it is the age at which children normally take a leap forward in their higher order thinking skills.) The experiment involved 220 children of this age. Half were used as a control group (to show the difference the experiment made compared to doing nothing different) and half were given two-hour sessions (with a break) of wild, organised fun activity involving things like games of tag. The sessions went on every day after school, for nine months (one school year).

> **Nigel:** *It's important to enable your children to have social interaction, and sports like football and sailing are helpful for this.*

Unsurprisingly, at the end of the year the children in the group which had the extra exercise were fitter and lost weight. But what was very interesting was that this group showed improvements in "executive function". This means they were better at blocking out irrelevant information when they were working on something and could **concentrate better.** They could also switch more easily between different tasks. Also, not all the children in the experimental group attended all the sessions, but those who attended the **most showed the biggest improvements** in test scores. The other children (the control group) did improve as well, but not as much as the children who had the exercise sessions; and the children who did have the sessions showed much more rapid improvement than those who didn't.

> **Philippe:** *As a lad I was very involved in sport, so naturally I encouraged my son to do the same. I took him swimming quite often and he played rugby at school for a while. When he took up karate, I did too.*

The conclusions from this study in the USA are supported by data gathered by the UK's Youth Sport Trust, a charitable organisation which aims to bring together a wide range of organisations, public, private and voluntary, to share experience and insights and work together to increase children's participation in sport both in and outside of school. Their figures show that at GCSE level 56% of students involved with the Trust's activities achieved five or more A*-C grades, compared with 52% of the students at schools not involved with the Trust's sporting activities.

> **Isabel:** *I introduced our girls to Tiny Tots (mini gymnastics) at the age of two, also ballet and tap. I used to walk every day to our village, as a matter of keeping me sane and meeting friends and also socialisation for them.*

In UK schools, most teachers are familiar with the positive effects of exercise – running around outside, getting breathless with a game of football etc. during play or break times. When the weather is bad and children are confined to the inside of the building, teachers often say children's behaviour seems to be worse during lessons – almost as if their moods and emotions are affected by not being able to "let off steam". Some schools deal with this by having exercise sessions and games indoors, and there are companies which will help with this as well as online exercise programs which can be used in the classroom.

INDEPENDENT SCHOOLS VALUE SPORT AND FITNESS MORE THAN STATE SCHOOLS

Independent schools in the UK have clearly recognised the value of physical exercise for health and fitness and perhaps also the importance for the development of young brains.

> **Carey:** *Exercise is useful because it wears them out! Also, otherwise there is a danger that they will always be plugged into their phones and iPads and other electronic devices.*

A survey of independent schools by the Headmasters and Headmistresses Association published in March 2015 revealed that a pupil in an independent school has more than 5.4 hours a week in activities related to exercise, which is more than double that in state schools, which according to a report published by the Youth Sport Trust is around two hours a week. Because of this, the Trust is working hard to try to improve participation rates (especially for girls) through grants and training, in liaison with companies like Sainsbury's and Virgin Active.

WHAT THIS MEANS FOR PARENTS

- The lesson is clear: if you want your children to do well in reading and maths, make sure they also have plenty of opportunities to **take exercise**.

- This doesn't mean you have to pay for them to join an expensive fitness centre. If you take them on walks in the countryside (or for that matter in the town) they will have the opportunity to run around and build up their fitness.

- Be a good role model – being a "couch potato" is not setting a good example!

- Find out what facilities, clubs and activities there are at your local Sports Centre

- Learning to swim is important for **exercise and personal safety**.

- Encourage your child to join sporting activities at school and praise them for it. (Personally, I've spent a few Saturdays on the edge of a freezing football field.)

- Most areas still have a public playground/park, completely free of charge to use. These have swings, roundabouts powered by muscles, balancing and climbing opportunities.

- If feasible, make sure your children walk to school, at least part of the way – maybe the last mile? Many schools have "walking buses" so that children can walk together and cross roads safely.

- If possible, **walk to local shops** instead of going by car. (I have been surprised how much stuff my small grandchildren can carry to the local charity shops when encouraged by the thought of some spending money.)

- Try and plan holidays which include **high quality fitness activities** – not everyone can afford skiing, but some caravan and camping sites have surprisingly good facilities for physical activities like cycling, hiking and water sports. Also, Center Parcs (if the cost fits your budget) is very much built around physical activities (no cars are allowed).

Chapter 8
MAKING THE MOST OF THE EDUCATION YOU ALREADY PAY FOR

THE SCHOOL SYSTEM WE ALL PAY FOR

The school system in the UK costs £88 billion a year (when including the local authority contribution) to run, and we all pay for it out of taxes, parents and non-parents alike. However, parents don't always realise that the role they play makes all the difference to the achievement and lifetime success – career and earnings – of their child. Some might even say: "I leave it up to the school – they know about education and I don't." More worryingly, a few parents seem to spend a great deal of time and energy challenging school staff, especially about behaviour issues (recall the head setting out her expectations under a Code of Conduct for parents that we saw above in Chapter 2).

WORK AS A TEAM

If a child sees her parents challenging the school staff's decisions and expectations, it's not hard to see why she finds it hard to accept teachers' instructions or decisions. The key point to remember is that parents and teachers

both want the best for the children, so it is critical that they **work together.**

> **Flora:** *Schools should get the parents to come to meetings to explain how they can help their children.*

There is no doubt that any teacher can tell you the difference that parents make when they play a full part in their child's education and support school staff. Parents need to take full advantage of the free state education provided because this can make all the difference to their child's future success. By working in partnership with their child's school, parents can ensure their child will fulfil her potential.

> **Elaine:** *I believe it is your responsibility to educate your children. It begins at birth, not at five. Schools should supplement what you do, not the other way around.*

PLAY PREPARES YOUR CHILD FOR LEARNING AT SCHOOL

Never underestimate the **importance of play**, which is the earliest form of **learning**. In April 2012, Ribena sponsored a report on the importance of play, reiterating the point of its critical importance to children's development and raising concerns that parents did not always see it as valuable and found it difficult to fit in time for play with household tasks and their jobs. The report also said some parents do not really know what to do as regards play with small children.

Play is how children start to learn about the world around them and develop important skills in manipulating objects and behaving socially with other children (turn taking etc.) This is why teachers of nursery age children provide a huge range of stimulating, hands-on and colourful activities as well as those involving music and rhyme.

Carey: *I used to incorporate numbers and colours and things when I was playing with my children – for example with Lego bricks.*

ENJOY PLAY

Spending time with your child playing with modelling clay, touching different materials and talking about how they feel, as well as singing nursery rhymes will help you to find out what your child likes, and will help you **build a good relationship** with her. Consciously spending time with your child doing something she enjoys is also a very important way of building her self-esteem. You are sending a message: "You are important." As discussed in Chapter 5 on speech and language, this also gives important opportunities to talk with your child – and not just about what you are doing.

Alex: *It's good to spend time with them, educating them, taking them places, doing little projects and playing board games.*

PLAY DOESN'T HAVE TO HAVE GOALS

The Ribena report quotes Sally Goddard Blythe, a consultant in neuro-developmental education, thus: "the danger [is] that adults see play as aiming to achieve goals. Play in itself is valuable. The most important aspect of it is the pleasure and the joy in it. When children have fun, they learn – whether that's the goal or not." The report also quotes Janet Moyles, an Early Years Consultant and author of *The Excellence of Play*: "Children engaged through their play in exploring the world learn to develop a perception of themselves as **competent, self-assured learners** who know that it's all right to ask questions, make mistakes and discover things for themselves."

> **Isabel:** *We played in our local park. I had good friends who also had youngsters, so we often met up in each other's gardens to play and chat.*

HAVE FUN LEARNING WHAT YOUR CHILD LIKES

So, if you plan some fun activities with your child, you are helping them to **prepare their skills for learning at school.**

WHAT THIS MEANS FOR PARENTS

- **Play prepares your child for learning at school.** Never underestimate the importance of play, which is the earliest form of learning.

- Even tiny babies have certain games they love – like the internationally understood game of "Boo!" where you hide your face behind your hands and peep out suddenly.

- **Talk with your child.** As already mentioned in the chapter on speech and language, play provides important opportunities to talk with your child. When they are a little older, it is not unusual for children to talk about things that have worried them – maybe at nursery or school – during play activities, giving you the chance to know about and deal with any issues. This is why play therapy is sometimes used to help children who have had difficult experiences.

- **Enjoy play and activities with your child.** By spending time with her, giving her attention and enjoying her company you will learn more about her interests and talents, which will give you extra ideas on how to help learning and keep her entertained. You will be surprised how much even little children can understand. It can also be great fun getting an insight into the way she views the world and will also give you a store of anecdotes to share with your family (and maybe embarrass her when she is older!)

- When you start to notice your child's **preferences and talents**, this then leads to ideas for other things to do with them to engage their attention and teach them (talking all the time about what you are doing!) Say you notice your child loves dinosaurs; this can lead to drawing and painting dinosaurs, dressing up as a dinosaur, pretending to be a dinosaur hunting other creatures, making a dinosaur cake and so on.

- **Have fun learning and preparing for school.** If you plan some fun activities with your child, where she can take the lead, you are helping her to prepare the skills for learning at school. It is particularly important to let her try things out and make mistakes – as Dweck says, "It's good to make mistakes; you are stretching your brain".

Darren: *I didn't know that having children was such fun.*

IDEAS FOR FUN WITH YOUR CHILD

There are many excellent videos on YouTube and Facebook pages with brilliant, easy and fun ideas for play activities with small children – including "messy play" using everyday items like cornflour and so on. Try search terms on Youtube like "Messy fun for children" and "Fun activities for little ones".

SUPPORTING ACADEMIC LEARNING AT YOUR CHILD'S SCHOOL

I will never forget a parent who was advised by his teacher that her son's reading level was below average for his age. She made it a personal mission to improve his reading and she read **every single night** with her child. Her son's reading skills improved by more than a National

Curriculum Level in three months – the progress which is normally expected over **two years**.

Most of what parents can do to give their child an advantage takes a commitment of time but not necessarily much money. Here are some of the key suggestions:

- **Work with your child's teacher** and school. See them as a **resource** and follow their guidance, and do what you can to support school policies, especially those regarding behaviour and expectations.

- **Read regularly and widely** with your child. Discuss what you read and ask questions to check understanding. Be encouraging and help them break down words into the sounds when they are little, so you can help them develop phonics skills.

Liz: *Communicate with the teachers above everything else; express your fears and concerns early, and try to understand your child is not the only one in the class!*

- When you read with your child, **discuss** what your child thinks of the characters in the book, what happens to them, and try to get your child to predict what will happen next.

- Find out **what topics** are being covered at school and help your child find out extra information, using the internet, heritage visits and the local library. There are no subjects being covered at any school which don't have some information somewhere on the net! The **skill of finding the right information** is just as important for your child's learning as the information itself. A key point of the learning is to **discuss** what you find out with your child, and ask her opinion about it.

- **Help your children with homework** – a controversial issue, I know. Parents, where both Mum and Dad are very busy working to pay the rent or mortgage, can feel a bit overwhelmed by expectations to help with unfamiliar topics or activities, especially as the children get older. Suddenly being expected to help your child complete a project on Victorian buildings or to complete 20 long-multiplication sums, using a method you've never seen before, can lead to stress and worry for parents.

> **Stella:** *I think parents could do with more encouragement from the teachers e.g. "I'm really pleased with how much you helped so-and-so with her homework." Parents need the positive too!*

- Use YouTube for some brilliant **videos** on how to use some of the new maths methods. Many of these videos have been created by nine- and ten-year-olds themselves. It is amazing how clearly these mini-teachers can explain modern maths in a way your child (and you) can understand. Also, remember that maybe there are others that can help – siblings, obviously, but maybe grandparents and other relatives.

- **Help** your child but **don't do the homework yourself.** If you do your child's homework for her instead of helping her, this could make it more difficult, as your child can learn not to bother too hard if she knows you will do it for her! You are also stopping her developing her skills in learning – not a good idea.

> **Philippe:** *As a hard-up student in France I used to provide a paid homework service for others in my school. I used to be careful to make sure the homework wasn't too good, or my customer's teacher wouldn't believe he had done it!*

Similarly, an enterprising young man of my acquaintance has obtained excellent GCSE results and has started providing paid tuition to younger students. Given that he is familiar with what is needed for a good grade, he can be confident his students should do well.

- There are expert subject teachers in every area who will provide paid tuition, and the best ones don't even advertise – they get new clients by word of mouth, based on excellent results. You can find out who they are from other parents or even the school's Facebook page. There are also agencies and online systems such as www.ieltsprivatetutor.com who can find you a local or online tutor. It is possible to have online tuition using Skype and there are even systems which allow the online session to be recorded so that your child can view it again.

- **Visit museums, churches and other places** to extend and broaden your child's knowledge. Many of them (especially in London) have become expert in providing a wide range of learning opportunities which combine learning and fun. Encourage your child to ask questions and talk about what she has learned afterwards.

- Become a resource to the school – **everyone has skills that a school will find useful**. Think of your family and friends as a resource to talk to children in the school: e.g. Gran can talk about her childhood and how things have changed to give an idea of social history; if you have an uncle who knows about joinery or carpentry, take full advantage of him for school construction projects, set-building for performances or design technology; if your cousin is a police detective, get her in to talk to the children. It is quite astonishing what committed parents from all backgrounds, skills and interests can provide to enrich learning in a school.

- **Travel as much as your budget allows**. Exposure to other parts of the country, other cultures and the world broadens children's understanding, expands their social experience and **makes them think**.

> **Darren:** *It's important to have experiences with them. Ours experience life as regards geography – they have travelled so much and had many positive life experiences.*

- Use the internet wisely to extend knowledge and learning. You can "visit" other countries all over the world using Google Maps. Even tiny children can benefit from a few minutes at a time when you start to notice what interests them. My small granddaughter was very interested in dogs, and a quick Google search for images of black Labradors (like ours) and Rottweilers (like her dad's) provided lots of opportunities for talk. YouTube also has some brilliant clips lasting a few minutes on everything from the current cartoon obsessions to Andrea Bocelli singing opera, or a baby kangaroo being born and climbing into its mother's pouch.

A FINAL WORD ABOUT YOU AS A PARENT

Finally, **believe in yourself** and your skill and capacity to ensure your child has the best possible future – as a person with good basic literacy and numeracy, and a healthy, curious, happy individual who knows the difference between right and wrong, and has a positive, optimistic attitude.

One of the most interesting conclusions I can draw from having interviewed a number of parents as part of my preparation for writing this book is that there are **many different ways of being a successful parent**. However, a number of those parents didn't realise that they had done a brilliant job, so I made sure I told them they had. This means that whatever the latest TV programme or parenting guide says, or the comments you get from your own parents or other relatives, **be confident**. Providing you consciously do your best, think about what you do as a parent and your child seems to be happy and making good progress, **you're doing fine.** When your children have grown up and you are enjoying your grandchildren, you will feel a deep sense of satisfaction seeing the results of your effective parenting.

Enjoy parenting – it is the most important job in the world.

Acknowledgements

Many thanks for your insights to all the parents and teachers I interviewed while writing this book, and whose views and comments are scattered throughout: Alex, Alice, Carey, Darren, Deborah, Elaine, Flora, Helen, Helen A, Isabel, Jenny, John, Karen, Ken, Lesley, Liz, Maggie, Nigel, Peter, Philippe, Richard, Russell, Stella and Su.

Thanks, too, to the numerous teachers and other educationalists I have worked with over many years, for their insights and expertise, especially Janet Darby and David Saunders who very helpfully read and commented on the final draft.

Thanks to all the researchers whom I have quoted and whose work has been made available on the internet.

Thanks to Suze and Lewis at Cavalcade, my publishers, for their advice and guidance in bringing this book into print.

Finally, thanks to my own children: Carey, Grace and Fred, for letting me practise on you... sorry that I didn't know about some of this stuff until you were too old to benefit!

Lightning Source UK Ltd.
Milton Keynes UK
UKHW051948220119
335798UK00007B/31/P

9 781999 62133